John Madden

Shall We Drink Wine?

A Physician's Study of the Alcohol Question

John Madden

Shall We Drink Wine?
A Physician's Study of the Alcohol Question

ISBN/EAN: 9783744670128

Printed in Europe, USA, Canada, Australia, Japan

Cover: Foto ©Thomas Meinert / pixelio.de

More available books at **www.hansebooks.com**

SHALL WE DRINK WINE?

A PHYSICIAN'S STUDY
OF
THE ALCOHOL QUESTION

BY

DR. JNO. MADDEN

PROFESSOR OF PHYSIOLOGY IN THE WISCONSIN COLLEGE OF
PHYSICIANS AND SURGEONS

"*The more concentrated the alcoholic liquor ingested, the more intense the inflammation of tissue. At the same time an equal quantity of the potable alcohols will sooner exhibit their characteristic symptoms if largely diluted with water.*"
—*Dujardin-Beaumetz and Audigé.*

"*Nothing, from the physician's standpoint, is falser than to think that the evil influence of alcohol is lessened through the increased substitution of beer for the stronger alcoholic drinks.*" —*Dr. Adolph von Struempell.*

MILWAUKEE
PRESS OF OWEN & WEIHBRECHT CO.
1899

Copyrighted by the Author.
1899.

PREFACE.

In the preparation of this essay, the writer acknowledges no motive but to discover the truth, and to put it in such form that it might be comprehended by the ordinary reader. As to the facts herein set forth, they are the result of the laborious, painstaking investigations of capable, conscientious, dispassionate men, and they rest upon the sound basis of experimental evidence. As to what may be the degree of perspicuity in which they are set forth, the reader must judge.

As to the importance of the alcohol question, there can be only one opinion. How long can we continue to increase the per capita consumption of alcohol at the rate of seventy per cent. every twenty years before it becomes evident to the slowest of comprehension that something must be done to save civilized races from annihilation? The writer believes, too, that it is the province of the physician more than the moralist, more than the philanthropist, and certainly as much as the statesman, to do what he may for the suppression of alcohol. This essay is, therefore, written certainly as much for the physician as for the intelligent layman.

In closing, the writer wishes to acknowledge the encouragement he has received from members of the medical profession, and especially the courtesy of Dr. A. Smith of Baden, who kindly permitted the use of much material from his valuable work.

JNO. MADDEN.

32 & 33 Sentinel Building,
    Milwaukee, May 3, 1899.

CONTENTS.

		Page.
I.	HISTORICAL,	9
II.	THE CONSTITUENTS OF ALCOHOLIC BEVERAGES,	29
III.	THE FOOD VALUE OF ALCOHOLIC BEVERAGES,	38
IV.	ALCOHOL AS A STIMULANT,	48
V.	THE EFFECTS OF ALCOHOL UPON DIGESTION AND ASSIMILATION,	66
VI.	THE GENERAL PATHOLOGY OF ALCOHOLISM,	74
VII.	ALCOHOLIC HEART DISEASES,	83
VIII.	ALCOHOLIC IRRITATION OF OTHER ORGANS,	89
IX.	EFFECTS OF ALCOHOL UPON NERVE TISSUE,	91
X.	THE INFLUENCE OF ALCOHOL UPON EMBRYONIC TISSUE AND HEREDITY,	102

CONTENTS—CONTINUED.

		Page.
XI.	ALCOHOL AS A FACTOR IN THE PRODUCTION OF INSANITY,	117
XII.	THE ATTITUDE OF THE MEDICAL PROFESSION TOWARD ALCOHOL,	128
XIII.	WHO BECOME DRUNKARDS AND WHY?	139
XIV.	WHAT IS INEBRIETY?	141
XV.	INTERMITTENT OR PERIODIC INEBRIETY,	144
XVI.	CONSTANT OR HABITUAL INEBRIETY,	151
XVII.	POPULAR FALLACIES REGARDING ALCOHOLIC BEVERAGES,	158
XVIII.	SHALL THE PHYSICIAN CEASE TO PRESCRIBE ALCOHOL?	174
XIX.	EFFECTS OF ALCOHOL UPON CIVILIZATION,	176
XX.	WHAT IS THE BEST MEANS OF COMBATING THE ALCOHOL EVIL?	202

TO

DR. N. S. DARLING,

OF LA PORTE, INDIANA,

whose abstemious, active, useful life is crowned, in age, by
a vigourous body and mind, this essay is
affectionately dedicated.

SHALL WE DRINK WINE?

A PHYSICIAN'S STUDY OF
THE ALCOHOL QUESTION.

I.

Historical.

The use of beverages containing alcohol is as old as civilization itself. In the countries of the East the mention of wine occurs in their earliest legends, and these give it a sacred character, attributing its origin to the Gods—Dionysus in Greece and Osiris in Egypt. The Hebrews credited its discovery to Noah, "The second father of the human race." Frequent mention of it is made in the literature of the Old Testament, where wine with corn and oil seem to be regarded as the choicest gifts of the soil and the highest achievement of ancient husbandry. Indeed, to produce wine in those times was an evidence of greater social stability than generally prevailed, for those ancient peoples generally lived and moved with their flocks and herds, remaining in one place only long enough to make one crop of corn. Those engaged in viticulture, however, could not be nomadic but must remain in one place to await the growth of their vineyards and the maturing of their wines. Hence they must have had the power to resist the encroachments of the universally warring tribes in order to have retained their vineyards and wine presses. Thus the making of wine was an index of a more powerful and stable civilization. Indeed, the cultivation of the olive and the vine required a so much higher order of civilization than the raising of herds and corn that the vine and olive became, with these ancient peoples, symbols of refinement and culture.

There is evidence that the art of winemaking originated in Armenia and other nearby localities of the East. From thence it spread westward gaining importance with the growth of civilization and commerce; and, while it had no place in the oldest Roman husbandry and was not used in the oldest Roman ritual, in the time of the Republic it had reached an important place in commerce; for it was artificially fostered by laws prohibiting the importation of foreign wines into Italy.

Probably scarcely less ancient than the making of wine from the juice of the grape is the making of an alcoholic drink by the fermentation of grains, notably of barley. Many hundred years before the Christian era the Egyptians practiced the art of brewing, afterwards it was done by the Greeks and Romans and ancient Gauls, from which peoples it has been handed down through intermediate generations to the present time. Herodotus writing about 450 years B. C. tells us that the Egyptians having no vines made wine from corn. It is probable, however, that the Egyptians were acquainted with the making of wine as well as the art of brewing; for the lands of the Egyptians were fertile and well adapted to raising the vine. Furthermore, the grape is mentioned so often by biblical writers, and was elsewhere so abundant, that the historian may not have been fully acquainted with the productions of that fertile country. Pliny also tells us of the Egyptians making wine from corn, and to this he gives the name of "Zythum" which is the Greek equivalent for a drink made from barley. Hellanicus, mentioning that wine was introduced at Plinthium, an Egyptian city, says, "From this source the Egyptians are thought to have derived their love for and use of liquor which they think so necessary for the human bodies that they made a wine from barley." The Greeks who received a great part of their civilization from the Egyptians, obtained from them also their knowledge of making alcoholic drinks from artificial fermentation of barley, in short, the process of brewing. Indeed in the writings of Archilocus, the Parian poet, we find that the Greeks of this day were already acquainted with the art of brewing. This was about 700 years B. C.

Again, from Aeschylus, 470 B. C., Sophocles, 420 B. C., and Theophrastus, 300 B. C., we also learn that the Greeks used a wine made from barley, not only for festive and ceremonial occasions, but also in daily life. Therefore, there is little doubt that the use of beer as a beverage is nearly as ancient as that of wine itself. Xenophon in an account 400 years B. C. in which he speaks of the retreat of the ten thousand Greeks, tells us that the inhabitants of Armenia used a drink made from barley. Dioscorides says that the Galatians also prepared a beverage by fermenting barley, like the Egyptians. Dioscorides makes mention of two kinds of beer but does not describe them sufficiently to enable a distinction to be made. He says that both were made from barley and that liquors of a similar nature were made in Spain and Britain from wheat. During the life of Tacitus, which was in the first century of the Christian era, in describing manners and customs of the Germans, he says that their usual beverage was beer and, though his description has many imperfections, there can be no doubt that they understood the method of making barley malt. The Germans not only made beer in abundance, but drank it freely. In Spain beer was used under the name of celia and ceria, and in Gaul under the name of cerevisia (Pliny's natural history, chapter XXII, page 82). Speaking further of the use of intoxicating drinks, Pliny says, "The natives who inhabit the west of Europe have a liquor by which they intoxicate themselves made from corn and water. The manner of making this liquid is somewhat different in Gaul, Spain and other countries, and it is called by different names, but its nature and properties are everywhere the same. The people in Spain particularly brew this liquor so well that it will keep good a long time. So exquisite is the cunning of mankind in gratifying their vicious appetites that they thus invent a method to make water itself produce intoxication."

The Romans are supposed to have introduced the art of malting into Britain. It is evident from Virgil that barley was known to the Romans for he speaks of it in the plural form, "Hordea." Pliny tells of the Hordearii Gladiatores, a kind of fencer, whose chief food was barley. The ordinary beverage of a soldier under Caesar was vinegar and beer. The former was very strong and was drunk diluted with water when on the march. Beer being so easily produced with an agricultural people with whom corn was plenty, and so suitable to the climate, it soon became a natural beverage. Before this time ordinary drinks of the ancient Britains were water, milk, and mead. The latter was a fermented drink made from honey. After the Romans were driven out from Britain the Saxons invaded the island, subdued its people, and from them learned the art of brewing. Various other savage peoples have made and are making beverages by malting different kinds of grain, or by fermenting natural fluids which contain sugar. Thus the Kaffir races of South Africa have, from remote ages made, and are still making, a beer by malting the seed of a variety of Millet (Sorghum Vulgare).

Natives of Nubia, Abyssinia and other parts of Africa also make an intoxicating drink by treating the seeds of the Poa, a kind of grass. Beverages have also been made from the juice of the palm, cactus, the sap of the maple, spruce fir, birch, and ash, the juice of the aloe and many other fluids. Indeed, there seems to be scarcely any substance yielding a juice containing sugar that has not been made to produce an alcoholic beverage by some primitive people to whom it was easily accessible.

*One of the most interesting subjects in medicine is the narcotic addiction of savage or semi-savage peoples. The making of alcoholic beverages preceded the white man's invasion of the countries of both hemispheres. The Indians of the Americas, the negroes of many parts of Africa, especially equatorial Africa, and the Malays of the islands of the Pacific, all had native beverages made by subjecting the sugar laden juices of certain plants, or a watery mixture of certain malted grains, to alcoholic fermentation.

In Central America and Peru *Atolle* and *Chicha* were made by malting maize flour, and in Mexico *Pulque* was made from the agave and also from the cocoa bean. Another drink called *Chocolatl* was made from the ripe cocoa-bean, which was first ground into a fine flour or meal. Next this drink was also fermented, we have reason to believe, for we read that the jugs of *Chocolatl* "with the froth still on them were never lacking when Montezuma made a meal."

The *Chicha* of the Peruvians, which may also have been used by the Mexicans, was made like beer from malted Indian corn. Narcotic herbs were sometimes added to it, after which it was called *Sora*, and the drinking of it was forbidden to many classes, especially the nobles and warriors. Drunkenness among the peoples of the old American Empires was widespread. Some Spanish writers

*See Prof. Friedrich Ratzel's "Voelkerkunde," or "History of Mankind."

attribute their early downfall to this cause, Peru especially. The Peruvians are said to have made themselves drunk with *Chicha* before entering battle with their enemies, but that instead of bringing victory brought demoralization. The early missionaries saw the evils wrought by *Chicha* in Peru and *Pulque* in Mexico and Yucatan and did what was possible to restrict their use. Finally the use of *Pulque* at the festivals of the gods was prohibited by law. The Peruvians celebrated a festival of the summer solstice during which even natives of low birth were permitted to get drunk on this maize beer, and "the days during which the festival lasted seem not to have been surpassed in wild debauchery by what took place in the temples of Ashtaroth and Hathor." The corn beer was made by the virgins of the sun, and was a noble offering. The first offering was made to the rising sun himself, and carried into his temple by pipes; "then the Inca drank to his ancestors, to the mummies in whom the sun-god had been incarnate, and lastly it was put at the disposal of the people."

The forest Indians of Central and South America also had their intoxicating drinks even before the discovery of America. These they made of Indian corn, cassava bread, the fruits of palms, and bananas. Still there were a great many tribes, especially in the southern part of South America, which drank only water and chewed the juicy stalks of plants. In Guiana pieces of cassava are put into a vessel and boiling water poured over them. When it is cooled, women chew it and stir it until it reaches the consistence of a thick porridge. It is then put into a long trough made from the stem of a hollow tree and water added, when it is allowed to ferment, the ptyalin of the saliva contributing to this result. When fermentation takes place it is strained through a reed sieve and bottled in gourds. The process is like that of preparing *Kava* in Oceania, and the finished drink is called *Paiwari*. It is yellowish brown in color and tastes like sour beer. In contains sufficient quantity of alcohol to intoxicate, and the Indian who attends a *Paiwari* feast is pretty sure to get drunk. The ordinary drink of the villages is unfermented *Paiwari*. A good deal of ceremony attends the preparation of *Paiwari*, as is the case with *Kava* in Oceania. Sugar-cane wine and another intoxicating fluid from a mixture of sweet potatoes and molasses are made by these people. In the latter fermentation is set up by the addition of chewed grains of maize, the latter acting as a yeast.

The inhabitants of the mountain regions of Colombia and Ecuador make a drink from fermentated watery solutions of raw sugar, which they call *Guarapo*. To this they add the juice of a small aromatic citron, giving the mixture a flavor not unlike that of lemonade. It is also drunk before fermentation sets in; it is then called "regular" to distinguish it from the other, which is called "*bravo*." A similar drink is made by chewing pieces of sugar-cane and spitting them into a calabash, and bottling the juice in a gourd, where it is allowed to ferment. The drink thus prepared is strongly alcoholic and intoxicating in small quantities.

Though the great tribes of central and northern North America had the sap of the sugar maple, birch, and sugar pine, and though they made quantities of sugar and were fond of it, they do not seem to have stumbled upon the process of fermentation. Not because they disliked alcohol, surely; for the Indian has always suffered great demoralization when he permitted his appetite to be gratified with the white man's intoxicants. Neither is there any evidence that the tribes inhabiting the cold regions of the southern part of South America have any alcoholic liquors.

Nearly all the negro tribes made an intoxicating drink of some kind, beer made from millet or Indian corn being the most common. They not only made the beverages but drank them to excess. Drunkenness among them was quite general, according to Wissmann, who advised travelers who intended to transact business with them to see them in the morning before the great daily drunk began. Beer of this kind was made both north and south of the equator, while in the equatorial regions there was an abundance of palm and banana wine. The Hottentots were an exception, and had no native alcoholic drink.

Among the Australians, the inhabitants of New South Wales made a drink from honey by a process of fermentation; but this seems to be the only native alcoholic drink among the people of the island.

The natives of the Samoan and other Pacific islands make fermented drinks from starch bearing plants and the juice of the palm. The Malays largely use a wine made from the palm and also a slightly alcoholic drink made from malted rice and the fermented juice of sugarcane. The Chinwans of Formosa brew a beer from rice or millet, fermentation being set up by rice meal which has been chewed by an old woman. In Borneo and Sumatra, however, the staple drinks are cocoa-nut milk and water.

That alcoholic excesses prevailed among the people of the earliest civilizations, history furnishes abundant evidence. The history of later times contains much that is more definite concerning the demoralization wrought by the immoderate consumption of alcohol; and no people, perhaps, suffered so much in this respect as the Germans.

Of drunkenness among Germans in the early centuries much has been written. "In order to still their hunger," wrote Tacitus, "the Germans need no fine preparations, nor do they care for delicacies. In their drinking, on the contrary, they do not show the same moderation. Should one undertake to satisfy their love for drink and furnish as much as they desire, he would find it easier to conquer them through their vice than by the sword." Also Venantius Fortunatus, Bishop of Portiers, thus describes a company of drinking gentlemen which he met on a journey to the Rhine and Moselle Country; "Singers sang and accompanied their songs with music on the harp, while around sat the listeners furiously drinking from large pitchers of maple wood. They drank each others health or for a wager; and any one who refused to take part in their debauches was considered an ass. One should consider himself lucky," continues the bishop, "to be alive after such a drinking bout." (Kurze Geschichte der Trinksitten; Dr. William Bode.) These drank wine and this condition of excessive drinking had then a long time persisted. We read that the German Emperor, before his coronation in Rome, was asked "Wilt thou, with God's help, keep thyself sober?" And only after the question received an affirmative answer did he receive the crown.

"Clergymen on the one side, and the gentry, judges, and soldiers on the other were often given to drunkenness," says Dr. Bode. The common people drank when they could obtain the means to purchase the intoxicating drinks; but the leisure classes above mentioned were about the only ones who could afford, at this time, the luxury of continuous drunkenness.

And wine and beer were held in high estimation. It

is related that Rudolph of Hapsburg, after receiving a drink of beer, much to his liking, from a burgher of Erfurt, rushed into the street waving the empty mug and shouting "Well in! well in! A good beer is that made by Herr Sifried of Bustade!" ("Wol in! Wol in! Ein gut bier das hat Herr Sifried uf gethan.") To be able to stand a good drunk was regarded as proof of a noble descent. Among the Hohenlohe vassals there was an old German custom requiring any one put to the test to drain the great feudal cup (Lehenbecher), which held a quart of beer, at a single draught, as proof of his fitness to serve the King. A similar custom ruled among the Alvensleben and other feudal peoples.

Things were scarcely better in the Monasteries, where the monks busied themselves with wine and beer making, in which they became famous. Frequent and excessive drinking was the result. In the French Cloisters matters were just as bad. In the famous correspondence between Abelard and Heloise, the latter complains of the evils of intemperate wine drinking. It pained her to see so much drunkenness and coarseness at the table. She quoted much from the scriptures and from the holy fathers of the church against wine drinking. Especially did she quote St. Benedict who says that wine is not a fit drink for monks. Still she could not think it right to have it completely forbidden to the nuns; because humanity had become so weakened and degenerated that they can no longer reach their ideals without some artificial aid. "It appears," she declared, "as though the world had grown old and that humanity had lost its original freshness of youth, as though according to the Word, Truth and Love had grown cold, not in many, but in all breasts. Since mankind has changed, the customs regulating human conduct should be changed or their rudeness moderated."

Abelard agreed with his friend. He thought that the nuns should either abstain entirely or have their wine mixed with water, one part of water with three of wine. Neither would he forbid drinking to satiety or an amount sufficient to satisfy without producing drunkenness; for "it is not satiety which is a sin but intemperance."

We also learn that in the Celebrated Cloister of St. Gaul in the tenth century, every monk daily received five quarts of beer besides wine in considerable quantity. In North Germany, also, intemperance was a greater evil than in the south.

Not, however, until the end of the middle ages did the drinking of alcoholic liquors become a national danger in Germany. As important cities arose and developed in North Germany, beer making became a recognized art and breweries sprang up in Einbeck, Braunschweig, Goslar, Hamburg, Merseburg, Luebeck, Danzig, Erfurt, Torgau and other places. There arose, indeed, as Dr. Bode says, a genuine "Beer Cultus" which reached its highest point in the sixteenth century. A learned Dr. Placotomas wrote, in 1575, in Erfurt "Five books in that Godly and noble gift, that sacred and wonderful art of brewing beer philosophically." A few years later there appeared in Vienna a "Wine book" by John Rosch in which the "wine cultus" was held in nearly the same estimation. To drink wine was here held to be a service of God (Gottesdienst). Drinking, revelry, debauchery, and all manner of coarseness reached its highest tide during the period just preceding the thirty years' war, at which time the German people were enjoying an era of commercial activity and material progress. One has only to read the satirical lampoons of that time to learn the extent of drunkenness among the leisure classes. Noblemen assailed each other with the vile language of the ox drivers (Ochsenknecht).

When Duke Henry of Braunschweig in 1539 called John Frederick of Saxony and other noblemen drunken rascals these replied that undoubtedly they were sinners in that direction, but that Duke Henry himself was even a greater offender for he could be found drunk early in the morning. "I will not excuse the life at court," wrote Luther in 1541. "Unfortunately all Germany is plagued with drunkenness. It is a bad old custom in the German land, which has grown and still continues to increase." The gluttony and drunkenness of that time are vividly described in the works of the Silesian poet, Hans von Schweinichen (1586), who went on a begging and drinking journey with Duke Henry XI of Liegnitz, through Germany. "These two Silesians were probably the greatest drunkards in that drunken century; but they had an abundance of company."

The sixteenth century has been called "the classical Age of German Inebriety." This, as has already been stated, was due largely to the prosperity of the ruling or leisure classes; but about the beginning of this century we hear, for the first time, complaints of the evils done by the stronger alcoholic drinks. In 1496 we read that the Nürenberg council was compelled to take action against disorders caused by the immoderate use of brandy, by forbidding its purchase on Sundays and holidays, and on working days only a half-penny's worth could be sold to one purchaser. In other places there must have been much drinking of brandy; for we find, for instance, that there were 34 distilleries in Zwickau in the early part of the sixteenth century. At the same time Frankfurt on the Oder had 80 and Zittau had 40. In Berlin brandy was allowed to be sold only in the apothecary shops until 1574.

Beer, however, continued to be the great national drink

and it seems to have reached a degree of favor with the common people amounting to almost veneration. Not only was it used as a beverage by all who could afford it, but it was also regarded as a remedy for various diseases. Many kinds were manufactured, not only from barley alone, but with the addition of other materials, and each kind had its peculiar use as a remedy assigned to it. We read, for instance, that rosemary beer was good for melancholia, "Scordien" beer was good for weak eyes, lavender beer "strengthened the head," sage beer "took away the trembling of the knee pan" and strengthened loosened teeth, and beer made from mugwort was good for unfruitful women. Beer was also extraordinarily cheap. For a few pfennigs, one could get all that he could drink. Three and four pfennigs a quart was the price of the best that could be purchased.

Not only were the German noblemen of this time drunkards, but their wives and daughters drank to excess as well. It is related that Henry IV of France, though certainly not temperate himself, refused to marry a German princess because he did not wish to have a wine cask constantly by his side. Among all the drunkards of that drunken century, Anna of Saxony, daughter of Count Moritz, was the most notorious. She had the doubtful reputation of being able "to drink all the guests under the table," and finally died of alcoholic insanity. It is related that her marriage with William of Orange in 1561 was celebrated by the drinking of 3600 casks of wine and 1600 barrels of beer. When Guenther XLI of Schwarzburg married Duchess Catherine of Arnstadt the wedding was celebrated by drinking the following wines and beers: 20 barrels of Malmsey, 25 barrels of Reinfall (a Welsh wine), 25 wagon-loads of Rhine wine, 30 barrels of Frankfort and Wuerzburg wine, 6 barrels of Necker wine, 228 barrels of beer. This was for the use of the guests alone; but besides this the servants and peasants received 1010 pails of "land wine" and 120 barrels of beer with which to drink the health of the happy couple.

Intemperance ruled all classes and both sexes, says Dr. Bode. The nobility set the worst possible examples. Only a very few of them lived thoughtful sober lives. Of the Saxon and Pommeranian nobles scarcely one was not a drunkard. Horrible things are related of them by Janssen. Count John Frederick of Saxony spent his time in arranging drinking bouts for wagers which often ended in the severe illness or death of several of the bibulous nobles. Count Christian I died of alcoholism. Christian II was also a notorious drunkard. When he visited the Imperial Court in Prague, in 1607, he prided himself that he was not sober a single hour during his visit. A foreigner once declared that his face was the face of a wild beast rather than that of a nobleman. Six or eight hours would sometimes be spent at the table. Now and then the drunken nobleman would make some filthy remark, throw the beer from a partly filled glass into the face of a servant or box his ears, or engage in some other form of drunken coarseness. As the court ladies constantly sat at the tables during these scenes it is easy to understand that they too drank and got drunk. The Duchess of Braunschweig was said to make a remarkable spectacle of maudlin happiness whenever she sat at the state dinner.

Citizens, laborers, and farmers emulated the conduct of the gentry whenever possible. The council of Nuernberg in 1540 provided for a hand wagon to go about the streets and pick up those who had become too drunk to walk; and in 1557 they deplored the fact that so many serious wounds resulted from drunkenness in artizans of both sexes.

In England and other countries at this time drunkenness was as prevalent as it was in Germany, and affected the same classes of people. The gentry of that time, from the fox hunting country squire to the prime minister, all drank to excess and the lower classes did the same when the opportunity presented. To write of drunkenness in England would, therefore, be to repeat the chapter on drunkenness in Germany for the same time. We have only to read the works of contemporary writers to obtain a correct view of the drink habits of the English people of that time.

Much has been said about the comparative harmlessness of wine and beer drinking, and that spirits drinking is responsible for practically all of the evils of temperance. This matter is fully discussed in another place. We can see, however, from history that unlimited drunkenness may result from indulgence in wine and beer.

There can be no doubt, however, that the introduction of whiskey as a beverage added much to the general demoralization produced by drunkenness.

Whiskey probably originated among the Celtic inhabitants of Ireland and Scotland. Its name is a corrupted abbreviation of the Celtic Uisage-beatha (Usquebaugh), meaning "water of life." Popularly, distilled spirit was known as Aqua vitae and was used solely as a powerful medicinal agent. It did not come in general use as a beverage until about the middle of the 17th century; and the first law of which we have any knowledge for the regulation of its sale was that passed by the town council of Glasgow in August, 1655. This act prescribed certain rules for the sale of "Ail and Aqua vitae." An excise duty was first levied on the "Aqua vitae" consumed in England in 1660, and in 1684 duty was paid on 527,492 gallons.

From this time on the consumption of ardent liquors grew with remarkable rapidity. At the end of the century the amount annually consumed reached more than a million gallons and forty-three years later it reached the incredible quantity of 8,200,000 gallons. With this rapid increase in the imbibition of strong alcoholic liquor, came great public demoralization. The liquor could be produced cheaply and its sale was practically unrestricted. This condition led to the multiplication of gin shops in London during the early part of the 18th century and so keen was competition that it is said keepers of these places put placards in their windows announcing that anyone might get drunk for a penny and that "Clean straw in comfortable cellars" would be provided for customers where they might sleep off the effects of the alcoholic narcotism. About this time the London authorities awoke to the necessity of passing laws to curb the destructive tide of debauchery, but the measures adopted (Gin Act 1736) were only slightly effectual. Acts were also adopted regulating the traffic in Ireland and Scotland about the same time; but here as in England they met with only a small success. Evasions of the penalties imposed by law, by smuggling, dishonest distilling, and the like, were incidents in the whiskey traffic then as they are now.

Comparing the drunkenness of the early centuries with that of recent times, it will be seen that there is less of brutal excess among the people in the higher and more responsible stations of life now than there was in the preceding three or four centuries. Not, perhaps, due to the fact that there is less alcohol consumed by these classes of society so much as to the influence on civilization which has softened the manners of all classes and given to all a much greater measure of self-restraint. What the per capita consumption of any of the European countries was, until very recent times, we have no means of knowing. It is probable, however, that in none of them was it as great as it is at the present time. The great mass of people were too poor to indulge, excepting on festive occasions, while at the present time some form of alcoholic drink is part of the daily diet of nearly all the laboring classes of Europe and America.

With primitive peoples the intoxicating effects of alcoholic drink must have been a deep mystery because of an inability to connect cause with effect. Unknown forces were ascribed to a spirit origin, to the gods, good or evil, according to their beneficent or harmful effects on man. With the Greeks wine found its apotheosis in Bacchus (Dionysus) the son of Jupiter. "He represents not only the intoxicating power of wine, but its social and beneficent influence likewise; so that he is viewed as a promoter of civilization, and a law-giver and lover of peace" (Bulfinch's Mythology p. 113). But the evil wrought by wine was recognized, even at this early day, no less than the apparent good; for did not the Princes of Greece undertake to prevent the introduction of Bacchus worship into their country "because of the disorders and madness it brought with it?" And did not Pentheus, King of Thebes, forbid Bacchanalian rites being performed within his kingdom, even going so far as to order the death of Bacchus?

This bit of mythology curiously reflects a division of public opinion as to the value of wine and its evils which persist, if we substitute all alcoholic drinks for wine, to the present day. This Grecian Apotheosis of wine is a part of our present heritage. Through all of the intervening centuries the industries concerned in the production of alcoholic beverages have grown and flourished with the growth of civilization. The drinking of wine has been regarded by all peoples as a proper mode of expressing the greatest human happiness. Is a child safely born to us, is a beloved daughter happily married, has a wanderer returned, is an enemy defeated, or has the Goddess of Fortune smiled upon us? Then let us be happy and give appropriate expression to that happiness by sitting down with our friends and drinking wine. Not by primitive peoples alone has it been deified. Great men of all times and nations have dedicated to it some of the best products of their minds. It has a high place in song and story. The literature of all peoples give it a place in a social organism made up of all such elements as make life complete and desirable. It figures in the profound solemnities of church rituals. It has been regarded as a food for the tender years of infancy, a staff for the tottering steps of age, an elixir vitae for those impoverished by disease, and a blessed nepenthe to soothe away the hours of grief or mental irritation. And ale has a literature all its own. For more than a thousand years the people of great nations have believed that ale gives health, manliness and strength; and the great masses of the common people, the nation's sinews in peace and war, have made it the one indespensible article of their dietaries. The god of beer, too, found a materialization in the person of Gambrinus, Jean Primus, or John The First of Brabant, the stout Flemish duke who is said to have invented lager beer.

Ardent spirits being of more recent date are not surrounded by the mysteries which surround wine and ale and have no god in any mythology; but many generations of physicians and influential laymen have given to the strong alcoholic drink an undeserved reputation for doing good. For many generations has it been used to stimulate a flagging heart, promote sleep, relieve pain, increase the vital capacity and protect the body from the cold of winter and heat of summer. Indeed, the giving of ardent spirits has, until very recent years, formed part of the routine treatment of nearly all classes of diseases.

Let anyone consider these things and he will understand why alcoholic beverages claim vested rights. They are a part of our civilization. Like a degenerate member of an imperial house ruling an unwilling people their evils are patent but they have hereditary rights. They have that authority which arises from an uninterrupted reign of many generations, they have social, political and religious prestige; and more than all, they have the prestige which arises from the ready command of uncountable millions of material wealth. Furthermore, the opinion prevails with nearly all intelligent people that used in moderation they are not only not harmful but beneficial in their action, and are only to be deprecated when used in excess.

Of drunkenness in modern times we know, unfortunately, too much. In our own country the per capita consumption of alcohol is increasing in an alarming degree. Statistics from the great nations of Europe show a like or still greater increase. Statistics for 1896 show that ninety million gallons of absolute alcohol was consumed in the beverages drunk by the inhabitants of the United States during that year. Furthermore, the average per capita consumption of alcohol during the decade preceding 1896 was seventy per cent. greater than that for the decade 1875-86.

This increase in alcohol consumption has been attended, pari passu, by an increase in crimes, deeds of violence, murder, suicide, manslaughter, and assault, while the number of insane to each hundred thousand inhabitants shows a like increase; for ninety million gallons of alcohol can destroy an enormous amount of healthy brain tissue. Something more effective than is now in force must be inaugurated to stem the tide of general demoralization or we shall be overwhelmed. Surely, however, the magnificent intelligence and practical common sense of the American people make them equal to dealing with this problem once their attention is sufficiently aroused to the dangers threatened by alcohol.

II.

The Constituents of Alcoholic Beverages.

The alcoholic beverages commonly drunk are wine, spirits (whiskey, brandy, rum and gin), and beer. Wine is produced by subjecting grape juice to alcohol fermentation, during which process the sugar in the grape juice is changed into alcohol and carbonic acid. The amount of alcohol in any wine will depend, therefore, upon the amount of sugar in the grape from which it is made. Wines made from grapes rich in sugar contain more alcohol than those made from grapes which contain a less amount of sugar. There is a limit, however, to the amount of alcohol that may be produced by this species of fermentation; for the process will not go on after the alcohol reaches 15-20 per cent. of the fluid. After wines are put in wooden casks, however, they become richer in alcohol, for a part of their watery contents pass through the wood and evaporate. They are also artificially "fortified" by the addition of alcohol. Some wines are not allowed to ferment to their fullest extent; they, therefore, contain a proportionately small amount of alcohol and large amount of sugar.

The following table from Dr. Weiss (Der Alkohol, Seine Wirkung und Sein Wesen) shows the average percentage of alcohol in the different European wines:

Rhine Wine	6–16
Mosel Wine	8–13 to 15–25
Red Bordeaux	6–13
White Bordeaux	11–19

Hungary Wine	9–15
Italian Wine	14–19
Red Burgundy	7–14
White Burgundy	9–12
Greek Wine	13–18
Port Wine	16–23
Sherry	16–25
Madeira	16–22
Cape Wine	18–23

The amount of sugar in different wines varies very much. In some all the sugar has been changed into alcohol and carbon dioxid while in others, like sweet catawba, the amount of sugar may rise as high as thirty per cent.

The principal acid of wine is tartaric acid, a constant constituent of the grape. Next in importance is tannic acid from the grape skins, especially in red wine. Acetic acid, an oxidation product from alcohol and succinic acid. Carbon dioxid results in considerable quantity from fermentation in some varieties of grape; but sometimes it is added as an artificial substance. Wine also contains oenanthic acid, which is a substance peculiar to wine and arises during the process of sugar fermentation. Wine also contains oenanthic ether which imparts to it its peculiar odor; but the "bouquet" is not due to this substance, according to Weiss, but to a number of ether like substances which are developed at the same time by peculiar kinds of sugar fermentation.

The inorganic substances in wine are potassium, sodium, calcium, sulphates and phosphates with traces of iron and chlorine, the proportion of each being dependent upon the character of the soil in which the grape was grown. Thus in Mosel, wine which is made from grapes grown on a soil of slate clay, may be found acetate of magnesia, aluminium chlorate, and other substances peculiar to that particular district. The total amount of inorganic matter varies from .1% to .3%.

THE CONSTITUENTS OF ALCOHOLIC BEVERAGES. 31

The proportion of alcohol, sugar, acid and water varies very much with different wines. Sometimes any one or more of these substances are added to those already in the wine to make it contain the properties usually found in a particular kind of wine.

Wine is much adulterated, the principal material used for this purpose being alcohol. Sometimes the alcohol used for this is impure, containing not only ethyl alcohol but also the heavier and much more poisonous alcohols, propyl, butyl and amyl. Unadulterated wine contains only the least poisonous ethyl alcohol. Various substances are added, also, for the purpose of coloring. Most of these are harmless; but fuchsin, often used for the purpose of coloring red wine, contains arsenic and may do much damage. The extent of this sophistication in Europe may be judged from the fact that the island of Medeira produces only about 30,000 barrels of wine annually, yet 50,000 barrels of Madeira wine are yearly exported to the United States alone. Our domestic wines are probably not adulterated to the extent that the foreign wines are. The abundance of grapes have made wines so cheap that adulterations would not be profitable.

Aside from wine from grape juice a great deal of alcoholic drink is produced from other fruits of various kinds. Apple, pear and orange cider, and wines from currants, gooseberries and other small fruits. In pear and apple cider the tartaric acid of the grape is represented by malic acid. In other respects ciders and fruit wines do not differ from those made from grapes.

All distilled spirits were formerly produced from wine. The brandy of commerce is still produced in that way and much is manufactured in the countries of Southern Europe, France, Spain and Portugal, and in the great wine districts of America, especially in California. It contains from 50% to 60% of alcohol, and the volatile substances, oenanetic ether and the like, found in wine. An artificial brandy is made from a 70% alcohol to which has been added oenanthic ether resulting from the oxidation of palm oil by distillation with potassium chromate and concentrated sulphuric acid. Brandy is also artificially made by the simple addition of oenanthic ether to alcohol diluted, or by distilling wine lees after adding acetic and nitrious ether.

Rum is made from sugar cane and molasses, alcohol arising from fermentation as in the case of wine, and formic acid resulting as a by-product. After fermentation the fluid is subjected to a process of distillation, the formic acid passing over with the alcohol. Rum contains from 60% to 70% of alcohol. It is artificially made by adding essence of rum, containing butyric ether, acetic, nitric, and formic acid, to dilute alcohol. Arac is made from rice by fermentation and distillation. Besides alcohol its chief ingredients are formic and butyric acid. Corn, rye, potatoes and other starch producing materials are used in the manufacture of whiskey. Each substance gives rise to a whiskey having its own peculiar character which depends upon the ether and volatile oils which develop during the process of fermentation. Whiskey contains from 30% to 60% of ethyl alcohol and a small quantity of the heavier alcohols. After remaining a long time in barrels these latter are said to have been removed by oxidation. This, however, has not yet been demonstrated, and is probably not true. Potato whiskey, much of which is manufactured and drunk in Germany, Ireland and other countries of Europe, is said to contain a relatively larger amount of fusel oil than that made from any other substance. Amyl alcohol, one of the fusel oil group, is much more poisonous bulk for bulk than ethyl alcohol, the relation which they bear to each other, being according to Dujardin-Beaumetz and Audigé, 8 to 1.7.

THE CONSTITUENTS OF ALCOHOLIC BEVERAGES. 33

The lethal dose of the various alcohols per kilogram of animal weight according to these investigations is as follows: Ethyl alcohol 8 grams, propyl alcohol 3.8 grams, butyl alcohol 2 grams and amyl alcohol 1.4 to 1.7 grams. It should not be forgotten, however, that the effects of the heavier alcohols differ in no way from those resulting from the ingestion of ethyl alcohol; the difference is one of degree not of kind. According to Strassman, also, (Experimentelle Untersuchungen zur Lehre von Chronische Alkoholismus) the amount of fusel oil is not more than from .3% to .5% of the amount of ethyl alcohol; in other words, an amount of fusel oil sufficient to make a 40% whiskey equal to one of 41 or 42%. Möbius and Weiss, however, regard amyl alcohol as being much more poisonous than indicated by Strassman, the latter declaring that a half grain is sufficient to produce narcosis and muscular weakness in an adult. Besides amyl alcohol there results from the oxidation of fusel oil valerianic acid and valerianic aldehyde.

Many other kinds of distilled liquors are made, some of which contain the volatile oils of different plants. All are no doubt more or less injurious; one, absinthe, especially so. This is made by distilling wormwood (Artemisia absinithium) with alcohol. In contains 60-80% of alcohol with the essential oil of the wormwood and is especially poisonous to the nervous system, being productive of attacks which cannot be differentiated from epilepsy. France is the home of absinthe, but the dissipated dwellers of all large cities of America and Europe have among them a considerable number of absinthe drinkers.

Adulterations of spirituous liquors are not infrequent. Most of these, however, are in the form of coloring matter, sandal wood, turmeric and caramel, which are harmless; not, however, so harmless are coloring matters from aniline and naphthalene which are also used for this purpose; and we have also heard of picric acid being used to color whiskey which was drunk by men subject to military duty to give them a jaundiced appearance so that they might be rejected by the military examiner. This substance as well as copper sulphate which is sometimes used to produce the green color of absinthe are both dangerous poisons.

By far the most widely consumed and most highly estimated alcoholic drink is beer. It is supposed to be made of germinating barley; but wheat, oats, rice and Indian corn are largely used in its production. The process of germinating produces a substance called diastase which has the power of changing starch into sugar, the latter being further changed into alcohol and carbon dioxid by fermentation as in the case of wine. Hops are added to the fluid before fermentation begins. From the malted grain is obtained dextrin, sugar, various salts and albuminoid bodies. The hops contain resin, tannic acid, a bitter substance called lupulin and volatile oil. Resin and tannic acid derived from the hops precipitate, in part at least, the albuminoid substances from the grains while the lupulin and hop oil remain in solution.

Beer, then, which is made from malt and hops alone, contains water, extractive matter, starch, gums, sugar, dextrine and albumens, alcohol, carbon dioxid, with a small amount of succinnic, lactic and acetic acids; salts, chiefly the alkaline phosphates and sulphates, pottassium carbonate, chloride of sodium and silicic acid. Aside from these at times beer contains a small quantity of yeast and fat.

More substances are used in the adulterations of beer than of any other alcoholic beverage, some of which are harmless and some the opposite. Unmalted grain, the husks of which have been soaked in lye, is sometimes added to save the expense of malt. From this beer acquires a peculiar bitter taste. Potatoes are mixed with the malt giving rise to fusel oil. Potato starch, dextrin, couch grass roots, carrots, beets and licorice are all said to be used to increase the profits of the brewer. Glycerine is also added as a preservative; but it destroys, according to Weiss, "double the quantity of malt extract." A small quantity of glycerine is a natural constituent of beer, but only .02 to .09%. It arises from the splitting up of sugar into glycerine and succinic acid. Glycerine, as is well known, in considerable quantity and taken for some time leads to serious disturbance of the digestive organs and the kidneys.

Substitutions for hops are of much greater variety, and as a rule more injurious than substitutions for malt. Any thing which will yield tannic acid in abundance may be used, the tannic acid taking the place of the ethereal oil and resin of the hop. For this purpose hemp is commonly used. This substance is well known to medical men as a peculiar intoxicant, giving to the subject pleasant hallucinations at first, and later producing narcosis. It is known as "hasheesh" among some eastern peoples. The use of hemp as a beer adulterant is not only attested by writers on the subject; but I have had this information verified by a brewer. The bitter principal of the hop is also frequently represented by such substances as orange peelings, wormwood, coriander, cardamon, mace, Salvacea clara, Ribes nigra, Ruta graveolens; but these are probably never, with the exception of wormwood, used in quantity sufficient to produce harm. Not so harmless, however, are other bitters used for the same purpose, such as gentian, catechu and quassia which with long use bring about serious disturbances of the digestive functions. Still more injurious are some of the materials which are said to be used for the purpose of adulterating certain foreign ales.

They are Solanum dulcamara (bitter sweet), one of the night shades, its leaves and berries, taxas baccatus, bark, leaves and berries, Datura stramonium (a night shade) the entire plant, white hellebore, the leaves and root, Colchicum autumnale, all parts of which are highly poisonous, and even opium. The above is certainly a formidable list of violent narcotic poisons which should be used only under the careful supervision of a physician. Strychnine producing plants, Strychnos nux vomica, Strychnos Ignatii, and Strychnos colubrina, are also used to impart the bitter taste to beer in the absence of a sufficient quantity of hops. All the members of the Strychnos family are very poisonous and extremely bitter. To the above really formidable poisons may be added, as occasional adulterations of beer and ale, colocynth, aloes, and picrotoxin, all dangerous poisons.

For coloring purposes the materials used are generally harmless. They are caramel, scorched malt, and extract of chicory. For the purpose of clarifying, however, sulphuric acid and alum are sometimes used, both of which are injurious to the stomach. Also through various manipulations before it leaves the brewery beer may receive an addition of alkali, yeast, sugar or alcohol; the latter not always free from a suspicion of fusel oil.

In spite of the fact, however, that so much material is used in the adulteration of alcoholic beverages, some of which is fatally poisonous in small doses, alcohol is the poison which inflicts by far the greatest amount of damage upon the organism.

It is highly probable that many of these injurious substances, by acting upon the digestive organs and nervous system, contribute to the general break down; but the most destructive changes such as interstitial inflammations, degenerations and the like, to which so many deaths are due, are clearly the result of alcoholic irritation.

THE CONSTITUENTS OF ALCOHOLIC BEVERAGES. 37

Malt liquors contain, according to Weiss, the following percentages of alcohol:

Munich beer, 4 varieties, an average of	4.3
Culmbacher lager beer	4.5
Porter	5.5–7
Ale	6.5
Vienna beer	4.0
Berlin and Thüringen beer	3.0
French beer	4.0
Pilsen beer	3.5

The average of American beers is probably about 4% of alcohol.

The amount of sugar in different beer varies very much, from 3 to 8.5 or 9%. The writer has found the German beers much richer in sugar than are those made in America.

III.

The Food Value of Alcoholic Beverages.

The most important food substance found in alcoholic beverages are sugar and dextrine. Sugar occurs in all the sweet wines in varying quantity and sugar and dextrine in malt liquors. The only other substance which can be regarded as a real food, found in sufficient quantity to deserve notice, is the group of albuminoid bodies derived from the malted grain and found only in malt liquors. Aside from these two groups of substances alcohol is the only material in the ordinary alcoholic beverages in sufficient quantity to be of importance as a food.

That alcohol is a food is asserted on every hand but still lacks confirmation. From the time that Liebig made his celebrated classification of foods until the appearance of a memoir by MM. Lallemand, Duroy, and Perrin, it was believed that ingested alcohol was totally consumed in the body, giving rise to vital energy. The investigation disclosed in this memoir showed that alcohol escapes from the body unchanged. Not only did they find that alcohol escapes unchanged, but that the products of alcohol combustion, carbonic, acetic, oxalic acid, aldehyde and the like, are not increased by alcohol ingestion.

In more recent times Bodlander (Die Ausscheidung aufgenommenen Weingeistes aus der Koerper, Pfluegers Archi., XXXII, P. 399 et seq.) expressed the opinion, as the result of his investigations, that about 90% of any moderate amount of ingested alcohol was oxidized in the body to carbon dioxid and water and that the rest, about 10%, is eliminated as such or as oxidized products of alcohol, through the lungs, skin, and kidneys. These results were afterwards corrected by Strassman (Untersuchungen ueber den Naehrwert und die Ausscheidung des Alcohols, Pfluegers Archi., XLIX, P. 315 et seq.). It was held by both that alcohol like every other carbohydrate should be regarded as a "respiratory food," that its oxidation within the body just like the oxidation of all other carbohydrats gave a definite number of caloric units and kept up the bodily temperature. In other words it was held that the kind of carbohydrate ingested was of no importance so long as its oxidation yielded the sufficient number of heat units to perform the necessary physiological work and keep up the bodily temperature. The fallacy of this method of reasoning is pointed out by Dr. August Smith (Die Alkoholfrage, P. 12 et seq.) who shows that as a matter of fact the most superficial observation will prove that it makes a great deal of difference whether alcohol or a like quantity of sugar is ingested, and that this difference is due to the difference in oxidation. Dr. Smith's observations upon this subject are so important that they are given here in substance.

Certain pure chemical observations which have been confirmed by physiological researches, but which have been neglected or overlooked in the literature of alcohol, compel a new interpretation of the action of alcohol within the living body.

Alcohol should be regarded as a respiratory poison, if the expression can be allowed, because it interferes with the interchange of the gases of the entire body by disturbing the normal life processes of the individual cells. This disturbance is produced by the affinity of alcohol for oxygen, on the one side, and its extreme diffusibility on the other.

In a general way we must assume that a normal conservation of the bodily temperature must be preceded by an equable oxidation process in such a manner that the material for consumption through a proper supply of oxygen shall be submitted to a properly regulated gradual oxidation, somewhat after the manner of a modern heating stove, the fuel of which when thrown in is not immediately burned; but, by an intelligently arranged draft, is made to do service for a definite time. The sort of coal which is appropriate for the stove's system may be regarded, in a certain degree, as the nutritious material of the stove, while other oxidizable material would produce neither warmth nor explosive force.

Without further argument we may assume that for heating our bodies a certain kind of carbohydrate is appropriate, that kind which would make no claim upon nor have no need for a greater supply of oxygen than that which is furnished by the normal process of respiration, both for the purpose of oxidizing the food material and removing the carbon gas.

A superficial consideration will show us that alcohol as a "respiratory food" does not answer the purpose of the first demand. We have, moreover, sufficient reason for holding that a double injury is inflicted by the oxidation of alcohol in the body: First, because the increased demand for oxygen cannot be supplied through normal respiration and, second, that as a result of the increase in carbon dioxid, resulting from the rapid oxidation of alcohol, the carbon dioxid cannot be promptly removed through expiration. We have, therefore, to reckon with an active and a passive kind of poisoning. The first arises from the fact that alcohol leaves the stomach in an extraordinarily short time, making a demand for an immediate large amount of oxygen which the normal respiratory processes cannot furnish.

The alcohol is, therefore, in part eliminated unchanged, but, for some time after its absorption, it must remain in contact with the tissues, awaiting a supply of oxygen or a removal to some organ through which it may be eliminated. The respiratory organs make an effort to supply the increased demand for oxygen, for the experiments of Zuntz (Beitrag zur Kenntn. d. Wirkung des Weingeistes auf. d. Respirationsproz. d. Menschen; Zeitsch. d. Med. 1887,S.I.) show that there is a reflex increase in the amount of air inspired amounting to 9% and by Geppart (Die Einwirkung d. Alk. auf d. Gaswechsel d. Menschen, Archiv. f. exp. Path. u. Pharm. 1887 Bd. XXII, P. 368.) the increase was found to be 7%. In spite of this reflex increase, however, the experiments of Wolffer have shown that the supply of oxygen is still insufficient to meet the increased demand, whenever alcohol is introduced into the animal organism. In alcoholized rabbits, with which Wolffer experimented, in spite of the fact that the gasometer showed they were obtaining a larger supply of oxygen than when other carbohydrate food was given, the respiratory quotient remained relatively higher, approaching or passing unity. Thus, for alcohol, the respiration quotient (i. e. for every CH combination there is a constant relation between the excreted carbon dioxid and the inspired oxygen) is exactly two-thirds ($C_2H_6O + 6o =_2 CO_2$ $3H_2O$), therefore the increase in the output of carbon dioxid is to be explained in two ways: First, that other carbohydrate of a higher respiratory quotient are oxidized with the alcohol, and this is the explanation accepted by Wolffer, in spite of the fact that his experiments were carried out with rabbits which had fasted for a long time, or, and this certainly seems the most probable explanation, the alcohol not finding a sufficient supply for oxidation in the circulating oxygen, must, from every tissue with which it comes in contact, take up the oxygen which is necessary to the cell in carrying out its functions.

The affinity of alcohol for oxygen explains the cell degeneration which is found in cases of acute fatal alcoholic poisoning. This degeneration is seen in nearly every organ of the body, but is particularly typical in the cells of the absorption vessels, especially those of the liver (Hankel, Vergiftung d. einmal, Genuss d. Alk. Vierteljahrschrift ger. Med. N. F. XXXVIII, I, P. 15, et seq.). So also have Nissl and Dehio shown this kind of cell degeneration attending alcohol poisoning, especially in the cells of the brain.

We see, therefore, that while the oxidation of alcohol within the body may give rise to a certain amount of heat, the circumstances attending its oxidation remove from it all claims as a food material. Still more shall we be justified in denying it food properties when we remember that the increased bodily temperature lasts for only a single moment. Within two or three minutes after its ingestion paralysis of the peripheral nerve endings cause a dilatation of the surface blood vessels, giving rise to increased heat radiation; so that though the total amount of bodily heat may for a short time be increased, the increase in heat radiation more than compensates for the increased production, so that the actual temperature of the body is lowered after the imbibition of even very small quantities of alcohol.

The amount of alcohol which may be oxidized within the body certainly must be small even under the most favorable circumstances; for, no matter how small the quantity taken, some of it is eliminated unchanged. Nor is there any definite evidence that the ingestion of alcohol is followed by an increase in the elimination of incompletely oxidized products of alcohol, such as acetic and oxalic acids.

THE FOOD VALUE OF ALCOHOLIC BEVERAGES. 43

Nor is the increase in carbon dioxid excretion by any means constant. The narcotic effects of alcohol upon the respiratory center soon decreases its irritability to such an extent that it no longer responds to the irritation of an increased amount of carbon, and the respirations become slower and shallower, further contributing to the general embarrassment of the vital functions. The reason why so many investigators have arrived at different results or why the same investigator has arrived at different results at different times, is probably due to the amount of alcohol given in the experiments. Naturally, we would expect an increase in the excretion of carbon dioxid when an amount of alcohol insufficient to narcotize the respiration center had been given, and a decrease in carbon dioxid excretion when a greater amount had been exhibited.

Dr. Adolph Fick, the celebrated professor of physiology in Wurzburg, gives the following estimate of alcohol as a food (Die Alkoholfrage, P. 5 et seq.).

"The oxidation of proper food material, albuminoids, fats, and sugar, has not for its principal object the generation of heat; but the maintenance of the functions of the muscles, the nerves, and the gland cells, in short, the activity of the entire tissues of the body. The animal organism is, in this respect, to be compared with a steam engine. If it is to do work it must be furnished with a definite sort of fuel put in a certain place through which mechanical power is generated; and at the same time, heat developed. Certainly alcohol cannot be regarded as an efficacious food for muscles, nerve cells, and the like. Not even in a narrow sense can it take the place of a force generating food stuff. It might be supposed that the heat generated by the oxidation of alcohol would be of value to the organic household, outside of the question of organic activity, in keeping up the bodily temperature in the colder surrounding medium. This, however, is not correct, and for two good reasons: First, alcohol greatly increases heat radiation by dilating the blood vessels of the skin, which becomes reddened through this increased blood supply. This gives rise to the deceptive subjective feeling of warmth, but according to physical laws the warm skin gives out more heat into the colder surrounding atmosphere, and the bodily temperature, according to abundant experimental proof, is actually lowered by the ingestion of alcohol. Secondly, the oft repeated statement that alcohol, when ingested, being much more easily oxidized than the tissues of the body, is burned up while the body tissues are spared. But this has not only been shown to be not true, but experiment has shown that alcohol actually hastens bodily tissue waste.

Although the oxidation of alcohol in comparison with the oxidation of true food materials in the animal organism is not yet completely cleared up, it is certain that alcohol in moderation cannot be counted as a proper food material. All the pleasant sensation of physical and mental strength brought forth by moderate doses of alcohol are deceptive and depend upon paralysis of the critical judgment and upon the momentary blunting of the sensation of fatigue."

The oft repeated statement that alcohol prevents nitrogenous tissue waste is by no means proven. Miura (Zeitschrift f. Klin. Medicin, 1892, vol. XX, P. 137.) in a series of elaborate experiments, referred to by Professor Fick, arrived at diametrically opposite results. He brought himself into a condition of what is known to physiologists as "nitrogenous equilibrium," that is he took just enough of a mixed food to keep him at a definite weight. Then he omitted from his diet a certain part of the carbohydrate food, and substituted an equal (isodynamic) amount of alcohol. The alcohol, however, did not give the expected protection; for there was proteid loss from the body, showing that the alcohol did not act as a food. He then resumed his old diet until a nitrogenous equilibrium was again established and again left out from his diet the same part of the carbohydrate material but did not substitute alcohol. During this period it was found that less proteid was lost from the body than during the time that alcohol was also taken, thus showing that instead of protecting the bodily tissues against waste by its oxidation, it exercised a directly injurious effect on proteid consumption.

Dr. Diakonoff of St. Petersburg (Wratch, 1889) carried out some experiments to show the effects of alcohol upon febrile patients which are of interest in view of the oft repeated statement that alcohol is a valuable auxiliary food, especially in typhoid fever. Of the seven patients subjected to experiment, six had typhoid fever and one exudative pleurisy. Five were moderate drinkers and two were total abstainers. The alcohol was given in the form of 40% vodka, in amount about one and three-fifths ounces of absolute alcohol daily. No other medicines were administered and the food was limited to white bread and milk.

He found that alcohol invariably lowers the assimilation of nitrogenous food and that there was no difference in this respect between the habituated and non-habituated patients. This interference with proteid assimilation was manifested by a largely increased amount of undigested albumen in the faeces, and unoxidized products in both the faeces and urine.

It has been shown, moreover, by Bunge (Lehrbuch der phys. und path. Chemie., Leipzig, 1889, P. 348 et seq.) that the carbohydrates are the chief source of muscular strength; and Mosso (Infleuenza dello zucchero sul lavoro dei muscoli-Ugolino Mosso and Luigi Paoletti) has demonstrated the stimulating effects of an easily absorbed solution of sugar upon muscular contractions. Certainly if alcohol has anything of food value in common with other carbohydrates its effects upon muscular contraction should be like those of sugar, in kind if not in degree. On the contrary, however, the experiments of Dr. Frey (Ueber den einfluss des Alkohols auf die Muskelermueding) show conclusively that the total capability of the muscle is very much lessened by the ingestion of even small quantities (two and one-half to five grams) of alcohol.

In the light of the foregoing definite experimentation and observation the reiterated statements so widely prevalent in authoritative medical literature that alcohol furnishes an easily oxidizable food which makes it of value whenever immediate vital force is desired or to prevent tissue waste in disease, should be at once and for all time discarded as untrue.

Returning to the subject of the food value of alcoholic beverages as a whole, the spirituous liquors may be eliminated at once as having no value; because they contain practically nothing but alcohol and water. Some wines contain sugar, varying in this respect from two or three per cent. to twenty-five per cent. or more. No one, however, will ever buy a bottle of the sweetest wine for its food value as long as bread may be had for five cents a loaf and sugar for six cents a pound.

We hear a great deal about the food value of beer and other malt liquors. Much is said of the highly nutritious "extractive" substances found in malted grain and held in solution in beer and ale. Many persons who make or echo those encomiums on beer forget, or never learned, that good bread possesses all those extractives. Moreover, beer as a food compared with bread is extraordinarily dear. In Germany where the best beer can be bought at the rate of four liters or a little over one gallon for one mark (24

THE FOOD VALUE OF ALCOHOLIC BEVERAGES. 47

cents), Struempell estimates that it costs about eight times as much as would be asked for an amount of bread containing an equal amount of nutrition, and that the difference is still greater in comparison with potatoes, peas, beans or other vegetables. He estimates that four liters of beer contain 240 grams of carbohydrate food and scarcely 32 grams of albuminoid material, while bread purchased for one mark contains 2,000 grams of carbohydrate and 250 grams of albuminoid food. In America bread can be bought as cheaply as in Germany, but beer costs the American consumer probably twice as much; so the American laboring man pays about twenty times as much for the food he obtains in beer as that which he obtains in his bread. Moreover, German beer is much richer in sugar and other extractive matter than that made in our own country, and is probably not adulterated to the same extent; for all beers made for domestic consumption in Germany are subjected to an examination by a state chemist, penalties being imposed upon the manufacturer if his product is not up to a certain standard, while in America no such system is in force. We may, therefore, without further consideration, decline to regard alcoholic beverages as foods.

IV.
Alcohol as a Stimulant.

From time immemorial alcohol has been used as a stimulant. The term stimulant has been rather loosely applied; but it is supposed to mean a substance which increases mental and physical capacity to perform work, to enhance, in short, the value of all vital functions, especially those of the heart. Exhaustion results from the lack of suitable food to renew the worn out tissues or from excessive work on the part of the exhausted organ, more tissue being consumed than can be supplied. An easily digested and assimilated food, with rest, are the prime stimulants when the heart's power is unimpaired through organic disease. Any remedy increasing the systolic power of the heart without increasing its frequency is the best stimulant when that organ alone is responsible for the exhaustion. In order to make plain all sources of exhaustion the fact that the heart's action is often notably depressed by a multitude of nervous reflexes must not be forgotten. One of the most common is that observed in the condition known as shock, resulting from severe injury, pain, or overwhelming mental impressions. In these conditions whatever will lessen the sensibility of the nervous system, will act as a stimulant. Here morphine and other narcotics act as stimulants by removing the reflex irritation which depresses the heart's action.

If the above propositions are well founded, and they seem to be, the value of alcohol as a stimulant may be determined by comparing its physiological effects with the requirements of a stimulant above indicated.

So many observers have noted a temporary increase in the force and frequency of the heart beat after the ingestion of moderate doses of alcohol, that the correctness of these observations cannot be doubted. The period over which alcohol exercises a stimulating effect upon the heart, is, however, very short; for, as has been shown by Smith (Loc. Cit.), it lasts only until the superficial blood vessels are dilated by the paralyzing effects of alcohol upon the paripheral nerves. The effects of alcohol upon the exhausted or fatigued heart muscle may be better understood after studying the effects of alcohol upon muscular work in general.

Exact experimentation to determine in what manner and to what degree muscular contraction is influenced by alcohol was first carried out, so far as I am aware, by Dr. Herman Frey, in Professor Sahli's medical clinic in Bern. His report was published in a pamphlet in 1896 under the title of "Ueber den Einfluss des Alkohols auf die Muskelermüdung." Mosso's "Ergograph" was used to register the amount of work done, from the time the contractions began until they ceased from muscular exhaustion, was estimated in kilogram meters. Experiments were made with the muscle in a fresh condition after a long period of rest, and after it had been fatigued by repeated contractions. Alcohol was given in the form of cherry brandy, cognac, wine, beer and diluted alcohol, the cognac and cherry brandy being also diluted, and in amount equal to from one and one-fourth to two and one-half drachms of absolute alcohol.

Upon the unfatigued muscle these small doses of alcohol, with only two exceptions, in one, that of a hysterical man, decreased muscular capability. Not only were the individual contractions weaker under the influence of alcohol, but the total amount of work performed before the muscle became exhausted was much less when alcohol was ingested. For instance, in one case the total work without alcohol was 4.66 kilogram meters; but, under the same circumstances, twenty minutes after drinking a little over a half pint of beer, the total amount of work was only 2.66 Kilogram meters. In a second case the total work performed by the muscles tested was 4.11 and 4.8 kilogram meters in two tests, while a third test made ten minutes after the ingestion of a little over a pint of beer, showed a total efficiency of only 2.63 kg. meters. A third subject gave 4.79 and 4.58 kg. meters respectively in two tests without alcohol, and only 2.02 kg. meters in a test made fifteen minutes after drinking about a half pint of beer. Several other subjects gave similar results. In one case the total amount of work was increased from 5.95 to 6.35 kg. meters to 8.6 kg. meters ten minutes after the ingestion of a half pint of beer. The author thinks, however, that this subject, as well as the hysterical patient, was influenced by suggestion. The results were the same whether brandy, wine, beer or diluted alcohol was exhibited.

A peculiar fact was to be noted during the experiments which explains the almost universal belief among alcohol drinking laymen, and among medical men as well, that alcohol gives strength. In spite of the fact that the maximum contractions were weaker and the muscles became fatigued sooner under the influence of alcohol, the subject lifted the weight without as much conscious effort after taking the alcohol as before. In the case of the author himself this difference was so marked that he was obliged to examine the apparatus to see whether some of the weight had not been removed, so much easier did he find the work after drinking a small quantity of alcohol, at the same time he was actually doing less than before the alcohol was ingested.

From these experiments, therefore, the author draws the following conclusions:

1. Alcohol has an injurious effect upon the unfatigued muscle, in that it essentially decreases the amount of work the muscle is capable of doing.

2. The feeling of fatigue is abolished by alcohol and, for this reason, the labor seems to be lighter.

The subjects of Dr. Frey's experiments seem to have all been men accustomed to a moderate amount of alcoholic drink daily. He remarks, however, that in his own case the effects of alcohol in decreasing muscular capability were most marked after six weeks of total abstinence from all kinds of alcoholic drink.

To determine the effects of alcohol upon fatigued muscle, experiments were carried out in the following manner: A series of contractions were inaugurated in each of which the muscle was completely exhausted, and the time between each series was so short (from one to three or five minutes) that the muscle was not completely rested before the beginning of the next series. The contractions thus produced, in a short time, a condition of complete exhaustion, finally rendering the muscle unable to respond to the stimulus at the end of the short period of rest.

When complete exhaustion was thus brought about the exhibition of the same small quantity of alcohol as was given in the experiments with non-fatigued muscle, enabled the muscle to make renewed effort. The total amount of work which the muscle could accomplish, after the subject had ingested the alcohol, was estimated by the author to be equal to the amount done before complete exhaustion by the non-alcoholized muscle; but in no case did the individual contraction after alcohol ingestion rise as high as they did in the absence of the alcohol. For instance, in one case the work accomplished before complete exhaustion equaled 3.35 kg. meters, when 15 grams of cognac were given. The muscle then accomplished 3.6 kg. meters before the occurrence of complete exhaustion. Similar results were attained in other cases. As a rule, however, the amount of work accomplished after alcohol ingestion was less than before.

It is to be noted here as a matter of much importance that massage had a similar influence nearly as great as that shown by alcohol, and the same exhibition of renewed contractile power followed the ingestion of 20 grams of sugar in watery solution. For instance, the total labor of a muscle before exhaustion equaled 1.95 kg. meters and after two minutes' massage was stimulated to renewed effort equaling 1.68 kg. meters. Similarly a case is recorded by Dr. Frey in which the total amount of muscular work before complete fatigue equaled 2.85 kg. meters, when 20 grams of sugar brought about renewed efforts, in which 2.55 kg. meters of work was accomplished by the same muscle before complete exhaustion again occurred.

By what means then does alcohol bring about renewed activity in the fatigued muscle? Not as a food certainly, or it would not have the injurious effects on non-fatigued muscle shown in the first series of experiments. Or if it has a food value, that is entirely smothered by its narcotic effects. According to Bunge (Loc. Cit.) the carbohydrates are the chief source of muscular strength. We would expect, therefore, that an exhausted muscle would be stimulated to renewed activity by the absorption of sugar. The effect of massage is not so clear. It might operate by increasing the circulation and thus enable the muscle to get rid of irritating waste products, and probably does act in that way.

Alcohol, however, has the power to both irritate and narcotize. Does it, then, affect the fatigued muscle by goading it to renewed efforts simply as a chemical irritant, or does it make further contraction possible by neutralizing the effects of tissue metabolism which are known to produce fatigue or, furthermore, does the small amount of alcohol given in these experiments of Dr. Frey lower, for a time, the rate of tissue metabolism, while it hastens the departure of waste products by peripheral dilatation of the blood vessels? None of these questions can be answered at the present time.

As to whether the fatigued muscle thus temporarily aroused by alcohol was thereby rendered incapable of performing the normal work of the unfatigued muscle, after the same period of rest, was not determined by Dr. Frey. He states merely that the alcohol seemed to have no deleterious effects.

Experiments were carried out with the electric current as an irritant, giving the same results as when contraction was voluntary.

It is entirely reasonable to suppose that alcohol affects the fatigued heart as much as it does muscles of the voluntary system, either by inhibiting the results of fatigue by peripheral narcosis, if the term may be allowed, or by spurring it on to renewed efforts simply as an irritant. That alcohol affects the heart directly and not through the central nervous system has been pointed out by Dr. David Cerna (Therapeutic Gazette, April, May and June, 1894). That alcohol stimulates by inhibiting the effects of fatigue irritation, is indicated by the experiments of Dr. H. C. Wood (Medical News, Vol. 57, p. 126) with alcohol in chloroform and ether narcosis. His statements are as follows:

"Of all drugs that which I think is usually most relied upon by clinicians as a cardiac stimulant in anaesthesia, as in other cases of heart failure, is alcohol. The chemical and physiological relation of alcohol to ether and chloroform are, however, so close that many years ago I became very doubtful of the value of this drug as a stimulant to a heart depressed by anaesthesia.

These doubts continually grew stronger from what I saw and read as to the effects of the administration of alcohol during anaesthesia, and were finally changed into conviction by the experiments of R. Dubois (Progres Medical, 1883), who found that in the animal to which alcohol has been freely given, much less chloroform is required than in the normal animal, to anaesthetize or to kill; or, in other words, that alcohol intensifies the influences of chloroform and lessens the fatal dose.

"In my own experiments with alcohol an 80 per cent. fluid was used, diluted with water. The amount injected into the jugular vein varied in the different experiments from 5 to 20 c.c.; and in no case have I been able to detect any increase in the size of the pulse or in the arterial pressure, produced by alcohol, when the heart was failing during advanced chloroform anaesthesia. On the other hand, on several occasions the larger amounts of alcohol apparently greatly increased the rapidity of the fall of the arterial pressure, and aided materially in extinguishing the pulse rate."

We might interpret these results by saying that, with a heart already narcotized, stimulation by abolishing fatigue irritation is not possible as it has already been abolished, and that the narcotic effects of alcohol would be manifest only in increasing the profundity of existing narcosis.

The beneficial effects to be observed from the giving of alcohol in conditions of shock, depend but very little, it is probable, upon its direct stimulation of the heart. The condition itself is brought about by some overwhelming impression made upon the central nervous system. Great joy, fear or other emotion is well known as a cause of fatal shock. On the other hand profound shock arises from purely physical causes, like the destruction of large sensory areas by extensive burns or the severing of the nerve trunks supplying these areas in high amputations of the lower limbs. In section of the optic nerve during enucleation there is a momentary profound shock during which the pulse disappears at the wrist. The amount of alcohol found necessary to bring about a reaction in these cases is much more than that which is found sufficient to raise arterial pressure. Those who have employed whiskey or brandy for this purpose will recall that two or three or more ounces may be given a patient before signs of reaction become manifest. It would seem, certainly, that the narcotizing effect of these large doses would have much more to do with relieving shock by rendering the nervous system unimpressionable than by stimulating the action of the heart directly. Opium and other narcotics promptly increase the action of the heart in the same way.

An abundance of experience under widely differing circumstances of climate, involving equatorial and polar extremes of temperature, have unanimously shown that the hardships of exploration, military campaigning, hunting, and all other adventures of like nature are not only in no way lightened by alcoholic ingestion but that dependence upon this so called "stimulant" has always been attended by disaster whenever the greatest physical efforts were to be put forth.

Experience in the army of the United States has shown,

according to Dr. Frank H. Hamilton, that the habitual use of no amount of alcoholic liquor by healthy men is to be advised under any circumstances. No exception should be made whatever for extreme heat or cold, rain or shine, nor whether the soldier had been accustomed to drink before entering the army. Even the moderate drinking of alcoholic liquor has been shown to be so injurious to those who are subjected to the hardships of life, in an arctic climate, that shipmasters, in the last ten or fifteen years, have absolutely forbidden the use of any kind of spirits to the crews of ships coming in polar waters. Nansen ascribed his successful journey across Greenland on snowshoes to the fact that he and his companions had not a drop of alcohol with them. The same holds good, but probably in a lesser measure, for tropical climates as has been shown by the experience of the British Army in East India. Moreover Karl Peters had a similar experience in East Africa. He says, in his work upon the German Emin Pascha Expedition, p. 268: "In Baringo the last bottle of cognac was destroyed. After this we had coffee, tea and cocoa to drink, and it may also be said that our health *became* excellent."

Certainly the proper test for a muscular stimulant is its use in just the hardships above enumerated. Failing to meet those requirements and indeed adding physical demoralization to the hardships already incurred, where is the ground for saying that alcohol is a muscular stimulant?

That alcohol promotes a "flow of ideas" is a postulate held by the majority of medical men. In the absence of definite proof to the contrary it is easy to understand that an increased flow of words might be mistaken for an actual gain in thought. By no investigators, as far as I know, has this matter been so thoroughly studied as by Kraeplin (Der

Physolog. Versuch in der Psychiatrie, Leipzig, 1895 and Ueber die Beeinflussung einfacher phychischer Vorgaenge durch einige Arzneimittel, Jena, 1892). The results of Kraeplin have been summarized by Dr. August Smith (Loc. Lit.) as follows:

"The action of alcohol upon mental processes, the results of which are so evident in acute alcoholic intoxication or drunkenness, as well as in the later stages of chronic alcoholic poisoning, deserve especial consideration. Kraeplin was the first to make the study of psychic processes of value in practical medicine, especially in psychiatrie. This he did after the method of Wundt, and we have him and his school to thank for a series of valuable conclusions as to the action of special poisons upon the psychic domain.

"Especially have we a series of his observations regarding alcohol poisoning which give us a very good understanding of the complicated processes involved, although a final determination of the same is not yet reached. The difficulty of arriving at definite conclusions is based upon the essential difference in the manner in which moderate quantities of alcohol affect the intellectual and motor centers.

"It has been proven experimentally that all the intellectual functions examined suffer a marked depression after the ingestion of small, moderate and large doses of alcohol, and that this depression makes its appearance immediately after the alcohol has been ingested, as a rule. In a few cases there appeared to be a short period of increased activity; but in these cases the amount of alcohol given was so small that this fact cannot be said to have been established. At the same time that the intellectual functions were depressed there was an increased activity in the motor functions which was followed, after a short time, by depression. Different psychic functions, in which motor actively played a rôle indicated these double effects very beautifully. When, for example, in the case of associations in which the reaction periods become shorter, that is the quantity of the associations increased, while their character became entirely different. Instead of the inner associations the outer ruled, instead of ideas connected in their logical relations, word memory and tune, rhyme and assonance became more prominent as is seen in cases of dementia in the human subject. 'More words but fewer ideas.'"

Kraeplin speaks of the results of his psycho-physical experiments in the effects of acute alcoholic intoxication and their relation to what is already known of the subject as follows:

"Let us again cast a look upon the completed picture of alcohol intoxication which we have attempted to develop by our experiments, and there can scarcely be any doubt that it possesses the same features which have become so well known to all of us through daily experience. The experiments give us the same appearances, though in a milder degree, which we observe in the brutality of the severe acute alcoholic poisoning. The difficulty of comprehension seen in the subjects of our experiments corresponds with the inability of the drunkard to follow the course of events in his immediate vicinity, and to properly conduct himself in relation to the same. This difficulty in arousing his attention exists in all degrees up to the point where there is complete insensibility resulting from blunting of all the organs of sense. In the retardation of the associative processes we again see the depression of his intellectual functions, the abolition of discriminative power which makes it impossible for him to impart or receive an idea, the lack of which makes it impossible for him to tell whether the idea is his own judgment or that of another, the poverty of clear estimation and insight into the range of his words and acts. The qualitative changes of the associations are signalized to us by the superficiality of the thought range, the tendency to stereotyped and trivial phrases, to empty jests, to foolish repetitions, sometimes in a foreign language.

"The stimulation of the motor reactions is the ultimate source of the sensation of increased strength, and also of all those thoughtless, purposeless, impulsive and violent acts, which has given alcohol such notoriety, not only in the history of foolish and thoughtless acts, but also in the annals of criminal impulses. It is the source of that lack of self-restraint which is seen in a company of drunken revelers among whom some catch word or some act may be the signal for all such purposeless and thoughtless reactions as foolish talkativeness, shouting, singing, screaming, declamation and the like; and corresponds to what our experiments showed when the difficulty of thinking had become marked. With this phase of alcoholic intoxication should be pointed out the fact that under its influence all psychic restraint, which is known to us as timidity, embarrassment and confusion, is abolished, that all those countless considerations which govern our conduct in our relation with our fellows, in the normal state, lose their power over us. We become courageous, unrestrained, and regardless of consequences, we speak without thought, express ourselves uncouthly without troubling ourselves as to the effects of what we say, and tattle our secrets nonchalantly alike to intimate friends or strangers.

This increased activity in the motor sphere and euphoria of the drunkard, Kraeplin ascribes to the subjective feeling of increased strength.

While Schmeideberg and Bunge look upon this motor excitement as the result of paralysis of the intellectual powers and would make the lack of judgment in the psychic direction answerable for all the purposeless motor impulses, somewhat like that which is seen in excessive ataxic movements of tabes. Kraeplin thinks it is due to the different manner in which alcohol affects the motor and sensory centers.

"We come, therefore, to the conclusion that alcohol, as a matter of fact, affects both sides of our soul-life, but each in a different manner. With large doses the sensory and intellectual as well as the motor functions are quickly paralyzed. Small doses, on the contrary, abolish only the first, while upon the latter domain the paralysis is preceded by a longer or shorter stage of excitement." Kraeplin also attributes a greater resistance to the motor centers against the power of alcohol poisoning.

What the euphoria of the drunkard most nearly approaches is erethistic imbecility. In both there is that naive self-glorification with progressive liability toward brutality, so much said by both drunkard and imbecile about what he has seen and experienced, and the same unshakable confidence in his own powers. In drunkenness there is a lack of the critical powers for which the extinguishment of the judgment is responsible, and I could without further discussion point it out as analogous to the foolish happiness of the weak minded.

Further, there can be no doubt that different centers of our brain possess different degrees of resistance. If we refer to the beautiful diagrams of Exner, it will be made clear to us, that those lines of action which are first to develop in the life history of the individual are for that reason the strongest and the least easily disturbed in their relation to others. It, therefore, needs no complicated theorem to demonstrate that the motor centers and those which control purely vegetable processes which serve to perpetuate the individual and the species, provide for the carrying out of their functions over established routes in quite a different manner from that of those centers the development of which is the result of social-ethical education which comes with more mature years. And, furthermore, that it is just these last developed social-ethical feelings which are first to suffer a blunting or complete extinguishment in chronic alcoholism is a well known fact.

But something further in this apparent opposition between the intellectual and motor sphere seems to me to deserve consideration.

That is the fact that with the cessation of psychic processes involuntarily the motor functions are set free. Sommer pointed out at the meeting of naturalists and physicians in Vienna in 1894, that in the Westphal phenomenon with the balanced leg, at the moment of the falling of the hammer in Jendressek's grasp a higher level was reached; in other words, that the energy which was applied to the hand grasp, probably because of the expectation effect through the attention being given to the hammer, at the moment the blow was interrupted, involuntarily it was transposed into muscular activity, which caused the leg to be actively raised for quite a long time.

The remarkable antagonism between morphine and alcohol poisoning seems to me to be a far reaching support for the presence of a law, also, for the conservation of power in the brain mechanism, where a sudden transmission of a cortical stimulation in some way seems to have an inductive influence upon the sub-cortical centers. As we have seen after the ingestion of alcohol there is an immediate blunting of the intellectual processes followed by an increased motor activity; but, with the ingestion of morphine in the abstinent, whatever increased motor activity may be present is diminished and intellectual capacity is increased. We have analogous phenomena in mania, in the excitement of febrile diseases with disturbances of consciousness, and others.

The experiments of Professor Kraeplin in showing the effects of small quantities of alcohol (one and one-fourth to two and one-half ounces daily, in divided doses) upon the psychic functions are of extreme interest and importance and conclusively demonstrate the injurious effect of alcohol upon the mental functions. It should not be forgotten that the amount of alcohol used by Kraeplin is just the amount which nearly every medical writer on the subject has declared may be disposed of without injury, or with benefit, by the ordinary adult, daily, if given in divided doses, properly diluted. In this manner it was given by Kraeplin.

The experiments extended over a period of twenty-seven days. Mental capability was tested in two ways, by problems in addition and by memorizing. The capability for this sort of brain work was first tested without alcohol and as will be seen in the figures, (1 and 2) with slight vacillations, there was a daily increase of efficiency.

The alcohol was then given when, for a few days, the mental capability remained at nearly the same level, then greatly and rapidly decreased, the decrease being much more noticeable in the case of the ability to memorize. After the breaking off of the alcohol there was an immediate rise of efficiency which continued for seven days. On the eighth day the exhibition of the alcohol was renewed and immediately there was a great depression in this form of mental capability. It will be observed by referring to the figures that the depression was much more rapid after the renewal of the alcohol following the seven days of abstinence. It would seem from these experiments that even this so-called small amount of alcohol first par-

FIG. 1.

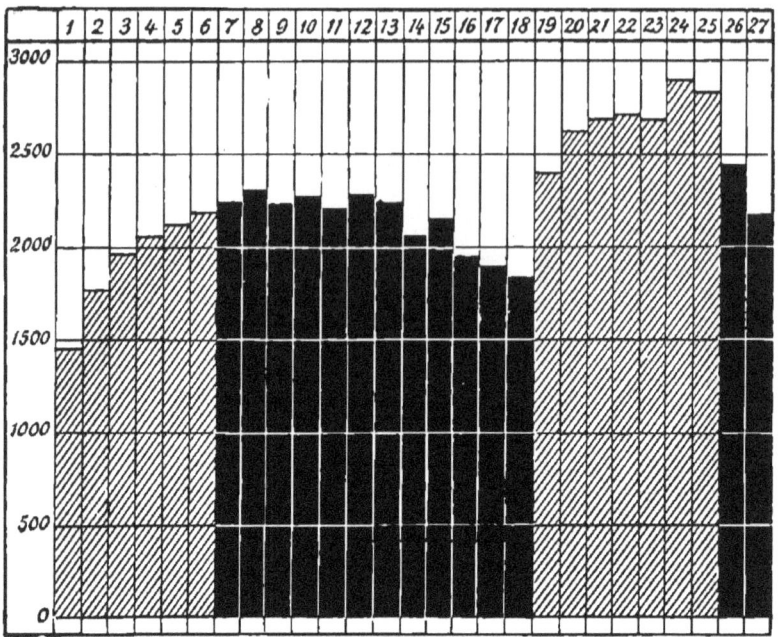

Exercises in Addition.

The black spaces represent the days upon which alcohol was taken, and their height the proficiency which the subject experimented with reached in the two mental processes. Figures to the left indicate number of Tests.

FIG. 2.

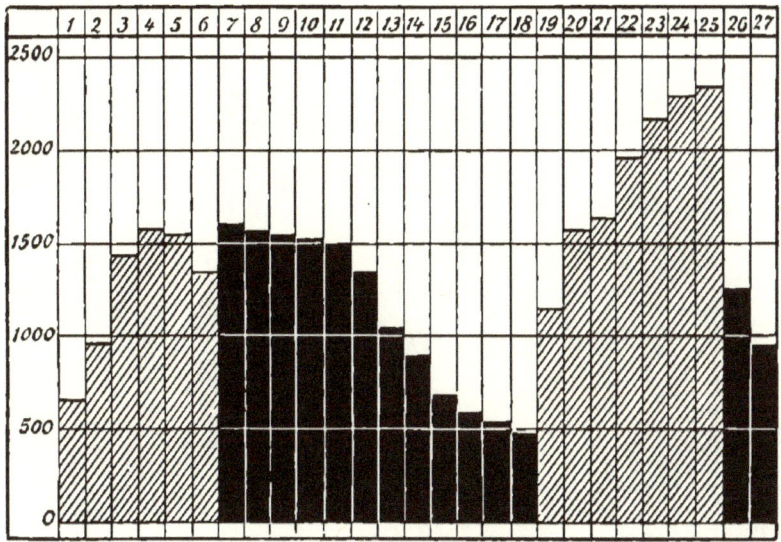

Exercises in Memorizing (Ad. from Dr. Smith).

The black spaces represent the days upon which alcohol was taken, and their height the proficiency which the subject experimented with reached in the two mental processes. Figures to the left indicate number of Tests.

alyzes the brain protoplasm, rendering it incapable of receiving lasting impressions in a normal degree; and that with continued use, the paralysis is followed by degeneration.

The same experiment was carried out by another investigator for a period of twenty-two days, and though there were individual differences due to various causes the same result was always observed, that is, an important lessening of mental capability during the ingestion of alcohol, and a relatively more rapid decline in mental cabability upon resuming the alcohol after a seven days' abstinence.

Another series of experiments were carried out to determine the effect of this amount of alcohol upon the length of the period between stimulation and reaction, with the result of showing that this period was always lengthened by the use of alcohol.

Still more significant were the conclusions arrived at through a series of experiments conducted by Dr. Smith himself (Die Alkoholfrage, P. 30 et seq.). He undertook the task of determining what mental processes were most affected by alcoholic poisoning. For this purpose he followed the arrangement of Aschaffenberg, which classifies mental processes as follows:

1. Internal Associations: Co-and subordination, casual dependence associations, predicative determination.

2. External Associations: Co-existence of time and place, identity, speech reminiscences.

3. Disconnected Perception Associations: Word-Supplementing or completion, tune and rhyme Associations, wholly unintelligible association. It will be observed that the first group of associations have to do with the judgment, the grouping together of ideas and drawing conclusions therefrom; the second has to do with the memory,

upon recalling matters in logical sequence, while the last is a mere matter of memory without judgment and without any logical sequence of events.

The following diagram shows (Fig. 3) Dr. Smith's method of determining the relative number of associations in each group estimated on a percentage basis. A total of 1,350 Associations was examined and classified. Examining the diagram it will be seen that the internal and external associations are almost equal, while those of the last group are so few as to be of no practical importance, during the period of abstinence from alcohol, 1-5 days. During the period of alcohol ingestion (40 to 80 grams being taken), extending over eleven days, the number of internal associations markedly decreased while the external group increased in the same proportion, and there is a relatively very large increase in the lowest group, those which have to do with disconnected memory associations alone. Again, when the alcohol is withdrawn there is a prompt return towards the normal relative number in each group, while a return to alcohol ingestion quickly decreases the number in the first group and increases the number in the other two.

A similar result was produced by an attempt to group a number of related ideas in series around a central idea suggested by a single word, or to describe a chain of external events and to name the circumstances relating to them in the order of their occurrences. For instance, when the subject examined abstained from alcohol the word "electricity" suggested a series of ideas like "continuous current," "interrupted current," "alternating current" and the like. On the seventh day, the first upon which alcohol was taken (in the same quantity as during the preceding experiments), the ability of the mind to suggest logically connected ideas decreased, and on the

FIG. 3.

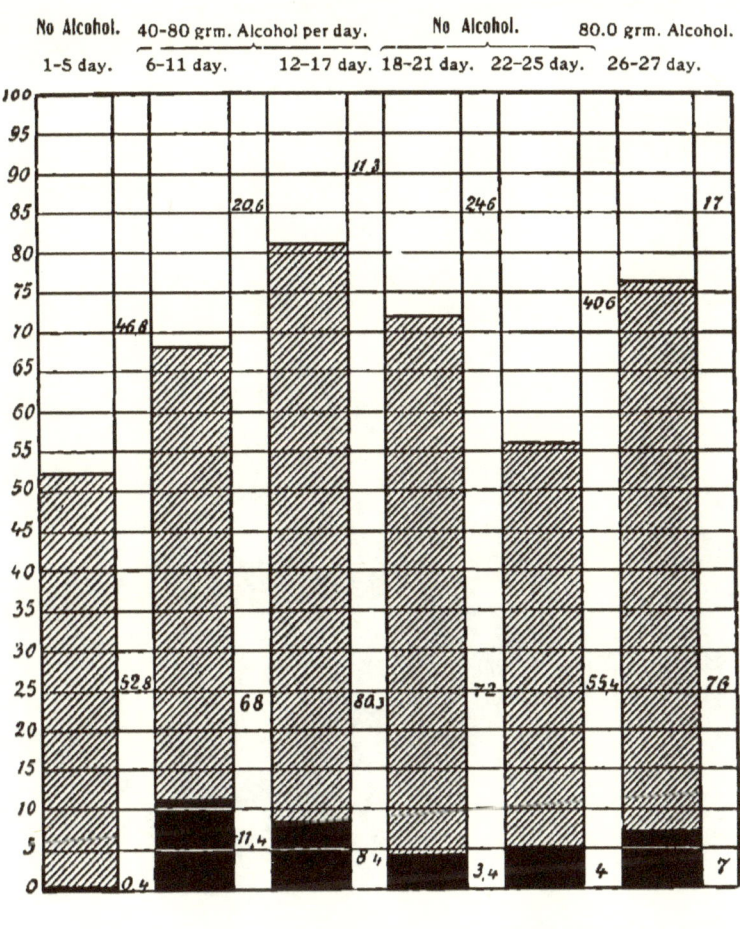

"Internal" Associations
"External" Associations
Associations not connected in logical thought,
(Rhyme, sound, word completion, and unrelated associations.)

No. of Associations examined, 1350.
(Adopted from Dr. A. Smith.)

17th and 18th days, nearly every central word suggested, not related ideas or words representing related ideas, but groups of words closely connected by a similarity of sound, (Unterbau, Baumeister, Meisterstück, Stückwerck, Werkstätte, Stettenheim). On the 19th day, with a withdrawal of the alcohol on the 18th, system in the associations returned as in the beginning, and a renewal of the alcohol on the 26th and 27th days again brought about the disconnected associations.

Taking those processes which lead to the formation of logical conclusions as the highest functions of the brain, which they certainly are, while mere word memory or sound memory is the lowest, the injurious effects of alcohol upon the quality of brain products, upon thought, is at once understood. Here is the basis, too, for the popular belief that alcohol "stimulates" mental processes because it brings about an increased fluency in words. It is a practical demonstration of what Kraeplin has already quoted, that acute alcohol poisoning makes "more words but less thought."

In the presence of the above definite evidence, but one conclusion can be drawn, and that is, the habitual drinker, no matter how moderate he may be, in his own estimation, in the use of alcoholic beverages, never reaches the highest possible plane of his physical and mental capabilities. Very interesting in this connection is a remark made by Helmholz, the greatest physicist of the Nineteenth Century, in a speech delivered at a celebration of his seventieth birthday. He spoke of the ruin of those minds which might have originated the most brilliant and original thoughts, and closed with the remark that in his own case "the smallest quantity of alcoholic drink seemed utterly to dissipate them."

V.

The Effects of Alcohol Upon Digestion and Assimilation.

The effects of alcohol upon digestion are two-fold: first, by irritating the mucous surfaces with which it comes in contact; and, secondly, by combining chemically with the digestive ferments, the products of digestion, or even with the tissues themselves. Added to the disturbances resulting from the above mentioned effects are those which arise from alcoholic narcosis.

The irritating effects of alcohol are manifested locally in the fauces, pharynx, oesophagus, and stomach, by the establishment of a chronic catarrh. The stomach suffers the most, for its lining membrane is the longest in contact with the alcohol. Catarrh produced by alcohol may be of all grades of severity from a slight congestion to a breaking down of the tissue. Post-mortem examinations in a subject dead of alcoholism show the mucous membrane of the stomach an intense red in color, thickened, with patches of infiltrated blood, and other patches covered with a tenaceous mucous. Indeed, so great is the irritation which may be produced that a suspicion of arsenical poisoning is often aroused, which is dissipated only after a chemical examination.

Not in the stomach alone, but in other parts of the digestive canal there may be intense inflammation. Here as in the stomach there is no limit to the inflammatory action of alcohol short of actual disintegration. Intense congestion first, the outwandering of leucocytes, dilatation of the terminal vessels with rupture leading to ecchymoses, suppuration and ulceration finally result. In a subject recently dead of alcoholism, I have seen multiple submucous abscesses extending nearly the whole length of the small intestine. Mackenzie states (Diseases of the Pharynx, Larynx, and Oesophagus, 1880) that the most cases of chronic catarrh of the throat come from excessive drinking of strong alcoholic beverages. Lancereux has seen ulceration of the oesophagus and Bergeret stenosis of that organ in chronic alcoholism.

Coincident with the anatomical changes brought about by alcoholic irritation are disturbances in the function of digestion. There are pain, nausea, vomiting, distress after eating, general emaciation and mental depression, the degree depending upon the amount of damage which the digestive organs have suffered.

Chemically alcohol interferes with the normal process of digestion, by rendering the pepsin inert as long as the alcohol is present, and by precipitating the incompletely digested albuminoid foods. The amount of chemical disturbance produced by the imbibition of alcohol depends upon the individual, the vigor of his digestive organs and his custom in regard to alcoholic indulgence on the one hand, and the amount and concentration of the alcoholic liquors ingested on the other. Something definite as to the nature and degree of chemical disturbances which a given amount of alcohol liquor of known concentration may produce was worked out by Blumenau in Koschlakoff's clinic in 1891 (Wratsch, St. Petersburg). The subjects of his experiments were five young men from twenty-two to twenty-four years of age, some of whom were accustomed to the daily use of moderate quantities of alcohol and some total abstainers. One hundred cubic centimeters of a twenty-five to fifty per cent solution was administered to each from ten to twenty minutes before a dinner consisting of five to six hundred grams of soup (one pint), a cutlet weighing two and one half to three ounces, and 6 to 8 ounces of white bread.

It will be seen from the above that the quantity of alcohol given varied from seven-eighths of an ounce to one and three-quarters ounces and that it must have been markedly diluted after reaching the stomach for not much of a pint of soup under ordinary circumstances would be absorbed in ten to twenty minutes. Assuming that only ten ounces of fluid remained in the stomach, the alcohol solution would have a strength of only four to eight per cent.

The effects of this quantity of alcohol thus administered were as follows: For three hours after the alcohol was ingested there was a very noticeable decrease in digestive activity; the general activity of the gastric juice decreased, lactic acid being practically the only acid present, while hydrochloric acid was almost wholly absent; from four to six hours after the alcohol was taken, digestion became more energetic, the general activity of the juice rose about 50% above the normal (from 0.22 to 0.35%), the proportion of hydrochloric acid also increased to beyond the normal (.12% to .14%), while, at the same time, lactic acid decreased and finally ceased to be present in sufficient quantity to give any reaction.

With the increase in acidity the gastric juice acquired an increased digestive power and under alcohol irritation the secretion of the juice was more profuse and lasted for a longer time than in its absence. During the first hours following the alcohol ingestion the amount of pepsin was also noticeably decreased as could be demonstrated by artificial digestion tests.

EFFECTS UPON DIGESTION AND ASSIMILATION.

All the changes above described were more pronounced in subjects not accustomed to alcoholic beverages, and strong solutions of alcohol produced more intense changes than weak ones.

It would seem, from these results, alcohol first paralyzes the peripheral nerve endings in the stomach mucous membrane as it does elsewhere, thereby rendering the cells supplied by them capable of secreting neither the normal amount nor kind of gastric juice. After the paralyzing effects have passed away, however, there still remains the irritating effects of the alcohol, and a more than normally energetic secretion of gastric juice takes place. Undoubtedly the presence of a strong alcoholic liquor in the stomach will retard digestion both by its effects upon pepsin and upon the partly digested albuminoids, precipitating the latter, which must be redissolved before digestion can again go on. These effects are, however, of secondary importance to the effects upon the nerve filaments. Significant, too, is the fact that the retardation was greater in the case of those unused to alcoholic liquor. If it were due solely to chemical causes there should be no difference between the abstinent and those accustomed to alcohol. Furthermore, the activity of the epithelial cells of the stomach was shown to be decreased in Blumenau's experiments from the fact that absorption was also lessened by the ingestion of alcohol.

The movements of the muscular wall of the stomach were also seen to be decreased in the experiments of Blumenau, which might have been anticipated, as those movements are probably the result of reflex stimulation of the gastric membrane.

Mohilanski (Medical Chronicle Nov., 1889) found that in those habituated to a moderate amount of alcohol daily, less food was assimilated during the days of abstinence than during the days upon which alcoholic liquor was ingested. In some cases the difference amounted to as much as 4.22% but averaged only 2.09%. With the habitual abstainer, on the other hand, the powers of assimilation invariably decreased with the ingestion of alcohol when given in quantity of two to five ounces of absolute alcohol in divided doses during the twenty-four hours.

Mohilanski attributed the increased assimilative power of the stomach after alcoholic ingestion in the habitue class to "an intensified gastric juice which resulted from prolonged retention of food in the stomach on the one hand and from increased digestive power and secretion of gastric juice on the other." A more probable explanation, however, is that in the habitue class, alcohol, or its irritating or narcotic qualities, from long continued use, becomes a necessity for assimilation as is the case with opium and other narcotics. It is impossible to see why it should not otherwise have the same effects with both the abstinent and habitue classes. He also found that nitrogenous metabolism always decreases. In thirteen of the fifteen persons subjected to experiment there was an average fall of 8.73%, the maximum being 19.42% and the minimum 0.14%. This decrease was observable when small doses were taken and was invariable with moderate quantities. No strict parallelism existed, however, between the amount of alcohol ingested and the amount of metabolic decrease. The decrease continued some days after the alcohol was discontinued. The decrease in tissue metabolism was attributed by Mohilanski to the action of alcohol inhibiting systemic oxidation, changing the blood pressure, dilating the vessels retarding the circulation, and thus depressing bodily temperature.

All investigators who have studied the subject agree

that alcohol interferes with the oxidation of fatty foods, much more fat being excreted unchanged after alcohol ingestion than during abstinence. As we have already seen alcohol makes such a demand upon the respiration and tissues for oxygen that the normal oxidation in all parts of the system is disturbed.

It will be noted that the experiments of Mohilanski by showing that alcohol, in decreasing the output of products resulting from proteid metabolism, seems to act as a conservator of the tissues; and thus warrant a conclusion opposite to that drawn by Miura. This, however, is not necessarily so. There are two sources from whence the products of tissue metabolism are derived, the food ingested and the tissues themselves. Anything which would interfere with the oxidation of the nitrogenous food, so that it would in part or wholly leave the intestinal canal unchanged, would necessarily decrease the output of proteid metabolism, while at the same time the various tissues of the body might suffer as much or more than they would during complete abstinence from alcohol. Practical experience has certainly demonstrated that alcohol alone in no quantity, either large or small, has the power of contributing to bodily weight in the shape of subcutaneous fat.

According to Wilkins (New York Medical Journal, Sept. 22, 1894,) alcohol precipitates ptyalin, forming with it an insoluble combination of the small amount of albuminous matter present. It also neutralizes the fermentative power of ptyalin, thus interfering with its physiological functions. In the small intestine alcohol especially interferes with the digestion of fats. It does this by coagulating the pancreatic juice, rendering it incapable of emulsifying the fats. This is one of the fruitful causes of fatty degeneration of various organs. The stearin of the fat is dissolved out of the fat globules, being aided by the duodenal secretions. The remainder of the fat thus becomes a foreign body in the circulation, and being a compound of palmatin and olein only, does not possess that property by virtue of which it is attracted to the adipose vesicle; but is deposited in the different organs, even in the ventricles of the heart and great vessels, thus constituting degeneration.

The glycogenic function of the liver is modified by the excessive use of alcohol, by preventing the rehydration of the alcohol, without its being taken up by the capillaries and put into circulation. This result is accomplished by the union of alcohol with water, which cannot be used in any physiological process, the mixture of alcohol producing a pathological result instead of a physiological one. The oxygen of the blood and water is prevented from uniting with the bilirubin to form biliverdin. Physiologically, therefore, even a small quantity of alcohol is inimical to life.

Before leaving this subject attention should be called to the fact that in habitual drinkers the vegetative and perhaps all other functions are stimulated by the presence of alcohol. Putting it in another way, and this seems the correct way to express it, with the habitual drinker, the absence of alcohol is attended by a decreased activity in all the physiological functions. This is simply analogous to what is seen in the habitue of any form of narcotic. In one accustomed to taking a considerable daily quantity of opium, its sudden withdrawal is attended by disturbances of every physiological function, sometimes of a gravity dangerous to life. The patient can eat nothing, digest nothing, may indeed be on a condition of physical and mental collapse. A dose of his accustomed narcotic promptly brings about a re-establishment of the, to him, normal order of things. He eats, digests, walks about, and talks naturally and cheerfully. Not that the physiological functions can ever be carried out to the highest point of efficiency under the influence of any narcotic; but the narcotic habitue establishes for himself a grade of physiological efficiency, the key-stone of which is the narcotic, which, if it be suddenly taken away, allows the whole artificial physiological structure to tumble to the ground. After a time nature readjusts the organism to the absence of the narcotic; but until that readjustment is accomplished the habitue will show less energy in all his functions than during the period of his narcotic ingestion.

The amount of disturbance following the withdrawal of an accustomed narcotic is, other things being equal, in direct ratio with the amount daily consumed.

One accustomed to the narcotizing effects of a few ounces of alcohol daily would undoubtedly exhibit a decreased assimilative power after its withdrawal. In fact just such results as those obtained by Mohilanski ought to be expected.

VI.
General Pathology of Alcoholism.

The key-note of alcohol morbidity is decreased tissue resistance, brought about by alcohol ingestion. The biochemistry of alcoholic tissue degradation is not fully understood; but it is probably based upon lack of oxidation and other nutritive disturbances. Of disturbances in tissue oxidation by alcohol, which has been so luminously explained by Dr. A. Smith, much has been written; Prout, Edward Smith, Harley, Schmeideberg, Vierordt, and other well known writers having contributed much valuable information upon the subject. More recently J. J. Ridge (Medical Pioneer, Endfield, Eng., 1894,) has discussed the subject in relation to haemaglobin as a carrier of oxygen to the tissues and carbon dioxid away from them. He has shown that under the influence of alcohol the time necessary for the absorption of oxygen by haemoglobin, as well as the time necessary for it to part with its carbon dioxid, is markedly lengthened. Undoubtedly this disturbance results, in part at least, from the affinity of alcohol for oxygen; but the irritating and narcotic properties of the poison may have some influence upon the cell life of the corpuscle, directly. Similarly, in all structures of the organism, it is not unlikely that irritation and narcosis play an important role in decreasing resistance, aside from that caused by the interference with oxidation.

Upon this same subject, Gaule of Zurich (Bulletin Medical, Paris, Aug. 25, 1895,) alluded to the fact that experiments upon elementary organisms had shown that alcohol causes atrophy by removing the water contained in them, and that the experiments performed in his laboratory, by Obersohn, show that alcohol has the same destructive influence upon cell protoplasm as is seen in ether and chloroform.

The decrease of tissue resistance resulting from alcoholic poisoning has been the subject of much investigation in very recent times, and the information thus obtained is of the utmost interest and importance as explaining the increased severity of bacterial diseases when the subject is a victim of alcoholism. In a series of experiments conducted by A. C. Abbott (Jour. Exper. Med. July, 1894), under the auspices of the "Committee of Fifty," he found that the normal tissue resistance of rabbits against the streptococcus of erysipelas is markedly decreased when the animal has been kept under the influence of alcohol, sufficient to intoxicate slightly, daily for several weeks. A similar, but not so conspicuous, diminution of resisting powers was exhibited against the colon baccillus (bacillus coli conimunis) under the same conditions. Against the bacterium of pus (staphylococcus pyogenes aureus), there were individual cases showing a decreased resistance when the alcoholized animals were inoculated in various ways. Still it.could not be said that there was a marked difference in this respect between the alcoholized and the non-alcoholized animals, as far as this particular bacterium is concerned. It is particularly interesting and instructive to learn that the results of inoculating the alcoholized rabbits with the germ of erysipelas bore a striking resemblance to the course of the disease observed in the alcoholized human subject. The effects of the erysipelas inoculations were not only manifested earlier in the alcoholized animals; but the disease ran a much more violent course, the abscesses being much deeper and more destructive. Abbott looked for structural changes which might explain the lack of normal tissue resistance, but found nothing in the way of macroscopic change which would throw any light on the subject. He believes that a closer examination might show some abnormality of structure brought about by the alcohol to which the cell owes its diminished power to resist bacterial invasion.

Such evidence as we have, however, indicates that the change is chemical rather than physical, as is the case in immunity.

Not only is the vital resistance markedly decreased by alcoholic poisoning; but the intestinal congestion thereby produced favors the outwandering of bacteria found normally in the intestinal canal. An inquiry into this subject was made by Wurtz and Hudelo (Bulletin Medical, Paris, Jan. 30, 1895), who found that intestinal bacteria are driven out during alcoholic coma. Rabbits were intoxicated with ethyl alcohol and killed when a profound state of narcosis was reached. In one-half of the rabbits killed micro-organisms were found in the peritoneum and blood of the portal vein, showing that microbes during alcohol congestion pass through the walls of the intestine and veins, as is the case in certain other poisons, cold, and asphyxia. They believe, therefore, that this diffusion of microbes plays a part in the production of peritonistis and liver troubles of alcoholism.

Very instructive in this respect is the establishment of an increased vulnerability to the cholera bacillus in subjects accustomed to alcoholic indulgence. During the epidemic of 1848 and 1849 Professor Adams of Glasgow estimated that 19.2 per cent. of the abstinent class died with the disease, while of the drinking class 91.2 per cent. of all attacked by the plague succumbed. He would, therefore, put over the door of every dram shop, "Cholera for sale here." During the epidemic it was further observed that most of the new cases of illness occurred immediately after a Sunday or holiday, which was generally spent in drinking.

Of the highest interest, in judging the worth of Dr. Adams' conclusions, is the result of an investigation made by Dr. Thomas in the Strasburg Clinic, as to the predisposing role of alcohol in cholera infection (Archiv. f. experim. Path. und Pharm., Bd. XXXII., Heft 1). He showed that alcohol increased the predisposition to cholera sixfold in rabbits, a result which closely corresponded with the observations of Adams on the human subject. Nor was this predisposition due to the gastro-intestinal catarrh inaugurated by the alcohol. A far greater degree of irritation was produced by such substances as Croton oil and cantharides, in other animals, without in any way increasing the predisposition to cholera. Moreover, alcohol did not lose its predisposing influence, even when solutions were used too diluted to produce any irritation of the stomach or bowels whatsoever. From these experiments it was decided that alcohol diminishes the bactericidal properties of blood serum, and that a small quantity of alcohol is effective for this purpose.

When the last cholera epidemic prevailed in Germany, the government sanitary officials advised the drinking of alcoholic liquors as a preventive measure. This advice was based upon the fact that the comma bacillus has not yet been found in concentrated alcoholic solutions. But, as Dr. Smith says, the comma bacillus has not yet been found in concentrated sulphuric acid, nitric acid, hydrochloric acid, nor strong solutions of copper sulphate any more than in rum and cognac, which articles might for just the same reason be recommended as preventives of Asiatic cholera.

In no direction is the tissue debasement of alcoholism more noticeable than in tuberculosis. The frequent occurrence of tuberculosis in alcoholics was long ago a matter of record. It was spoken of by physicians of the last century and has been confirmed beyond doubt by numerous observers during the past twenty-five years. Lancereaux (Le Bulletin Medical, March 6, 1895,) declares that he has held this opinion for more than thirty years. He could, he says, produce many proofs to support it. The phthisis of drunkards is peculiar. Instead of first involving the front of the left apex, which is the classical site for its commencement, when it results from insufficient aeration or nutrition it attacks the right apex posteriorly, producing lessening of elasticity on percussion. It is also different in its evolution, for the disease generally improves after the first attack, and the patient frequently recovers, if he give up his bad habits and properly nourish himself, even though the disease may have been attended by hemorrhages. This, however, he rarely does. A second and a third attack follows, converting the first attack into an alarming condition due to the dissemination of the tubercles. In some cases this dissemination is general from the beginning; but, even in these cases treatment may meet with success and the process be arrested. In other drunkards tuberculosis simultaneously affects the lungs, meninges of the brain and the peritoneum, quickly causing death. This phenomenon he has often seen in market-porters, coopers, and truckmen. In all cases, he believes, alcohols and essential oils, by diminishing organic combustion and being eliminated by the lungs, create at the same time a general and local predisposition which furnishes a proper field for the growth of tubercle bacilli.

Lancereaux further contributed (Bulletin Medical, June 26, 1895,) valuable evidence in support of these views by showing that the increase in tuberculosis is in proportion to the increase in alcoholic consumption. Alcoholism did not become notable in France until after the vines had been destroyed by the phylloxera. At that time pulmonary consumption was met with in men only one half as often as in women. At the present time twice as many men as women are afflicted, because the women of France, as a rule, are not habituated to the use of excessive quantities of alcohol.

Legrain also (Medical Press & Circular, London, Jan. 13, 1894,) speaks of having observed 55 cases of tuberculosis in 819 descendants of 215 cases of alcoholic parentage.

T. D. Crothers (Journal of Am. Med. Assn. Apr. 9, 1898,) takes the ground that alcoholic inebriety and tuberculosis are allied diseases. He says that in some families the two conditions alternate. Some of the members drink to great excess, then abstain, contract tuberculosis, and die. Others have all the signs of consumption when they begin to drink and recover it, but become inebriates afterward, and die suddenly of acute pneumonia or nephritis. Instances of the former class are very common, and in these the course of the disease is very rapid. In the case of the latter class alcohol seems to abort the tuberculosis in some cases while in others it makes the progress of the disease more rapid.

In his experience with 2,000 cases fully twenty per cent. were associated with tuberculosis; but a much larger percentage of all cases of alcoholic inebriety die from tuberculosis, "of which, probably, there was no intimation until the end of life." Close observers know that these cases have a heredity and a great variety of symptoms in common. The phthisical insanities mentioned by Dr. Maudsley, inherit qualities which lead first to inebriety and later to the development of tuberculosis. Insanity sometimes develops in these cases; but is not so frequent as tuberculosis; and, when it does occur, it is usually traceable to some injury like sunstroke or mental strain. Physical and mental unrest due to inherited degeneracy drive the victim to the narcotic effects of alcohol for relief; but inebriety, producing a still greater degree of degeneracy, prepares the subject for tuberculosis provided degeneracy has not taken on acute forms in other centres leading to inflammation.

The production of bronchial catarrhs by alcoholic drinking lead in the same way to the invasion of tuberculosis. Dr. Sharkey in The Journal of the London Pathological Society is quoted as saying that disturbances and lesions of the vagus were such as may come from alcoholism, by lowering the nutrition of the lung, and prepare it to become the nidus of the tubercle bacillus. Reference is also made to the exhaustive paper of Dr. Alison (in Archives Generales de Medicine) relative to tuberculosis in alcoholics. In the study of eighteen hundred cases he reached the positive conclusion that alcohol predisposed subjects to tuberculosis both by producing a local irritation and lowering the general vitality. He believes that inebriety and tuberculosis are interchangeable, both following from the same general cause and producing death by the latter before the age of forty. After that age acute inflammations are more common.

Reference is also made to the writings of Dr. Mays in the Journal of Inebriety for 1889, Dr. Irwell, in "Race Deterioration," Dr. Williams in his work on Pulmonary Consumption, Dr. Clouston of Edinborough and Dr. Payne in "Pathology of Chronic Alcoholism." The evidence given by these writers is corroborative. In all of them the relation of alcoholism and tuberculosis is confirmed by numerous observations, and the part played by heredity in producing alcoholic inebriates from phthisical parents and consumptives from alcoholic parents is referred to at length.

To these I could add numerous cases in my own experience, two of them occurring within the past few months. The first was a nervous, erratic man of 36 years of age, possessing a restless energy and given to frequent outbursts of passionate rage. His heredity was bad, his father having been an alcoholic, and several brothers and sisters died in infancy. He had been addicted to the use of large quantities of alcoholic liquors, chiefly in the form of strong spirits, but married and gave up alcohol entirely. About this time he had a bronchial catarrh but no evidence of tuberculosis. Soon, however, the characteristic symptoms developed and he died in a few months of pulmonary consumption.

The other was a young man of 32. He had been a hard drinker for ten years or more; but finally "graduated" from a local institution for drunkards and became a total abstainer. His health was only fair after this and began to fail in a few months, chiefly because of digestive disturbances. This was in September. In January following there was complete infiltration of the right lung, with cavities of the apex. An attack of pneumonia supervened in February, and the already rapid course of the disease was made still more rapid, death occurring on the first of March. What the hereditary influences in this case were, as regards alcohol, I do not know, but there was no history of tuberculosis.

Several other similar cases occur to me as I write these. In some of them there was a history of heredity alcoholism or consumption or both, while in others pulmonary consumption cut short a life the greater part of which had been spent in alcoholic dissipation. None of these cases, however, as I recall them, present any special features not already mentioned. They would be simply in the nature of corroborative testimony.

VII.

Alcoholic Heart Diseases.

In the healthy subject death results from failure of respiration, when a lethal dose of alcohol is taken, through narcosis of the respiratory center of the medulla. Death may result, however, from heart exhaustion due, no doubt, to the irritating effects of alcohol, when large doses are ingested at short intervals, but not sufficient in quantity to produce profound narcosis. This form of alcohol poisoning is often seen in subjects who tolerate enormous quantities of alcohol without being sufficiently narcotized thereby to produce prolonged sleep, death usually occurring at the end of a prolonged spree attended by evidence of great nervous excitement.

There is no doubt that alcohol acts directly upon the heart to produce its irritating effects, and there is good reason for believing that when death results from heart failure due to alcohol it is brought about by the direct poisoning of the heart muscle or its ganglia. I have seen five cases resulting fatally in which no organic change in the heart could be made out during life; and, in two of these, post-mortem examinations showed no changes in the heart muscle sufficient to account for the fatal termination. Yet, in all of these, death was sudden and followed a debauch in which great quantities of alcohol were drunk. Two of these cases, the two upon whom post-mortems were held, are so instructive and seem to so fully confirm the belief that death may result from sheer heart exhaustion due to the long continued irritant action of alcohol that I shall quote them in full:

M. J., a man 43 years of age, large, muscular, well nourished, and had never had any serious illness. His social status was good and he held a municipal office of considerable importance. He consulted me in the latter part of November, just after or during a debauch of two or three weeks, during which time he drank large quantities of strong liquor. At this time his most marked symptom was a very rapid and feeble pulse, so rapid that it was almost impossible to count it and so feeble that the entire surface of his body was cyanotic. Upon careful examination, no organic change in any of the chest organs could be made out; but there was a moderate amount of albumen in the urine. He did not make a rapid recovery; but about the first of the following March his heart was apparently normal in all respects, albumen disappeared, and he declared he felt as well as he ever did. During the last days of the following May he again began to drink excessively, and continued his excesses for nearly two weeks. I saw him again at this time and he presented a condition identical with that of the preceding autumn. A day or two afterwards, while attempting to sit in a chair, he fell over and expired suddenly.

Post-mortem examination disclosed the usual irritation due to drunkenness but not in a marked degree; for, at the time of his death, he had had no alcohol for three days. The heart was not dilated. It had, however, a sodden intensely red appearance and a few pigmented points due to the deposition of broken down blood corpuscles.

The second case, W. G. G., male, 29 years old, a traveling salesman in easy financial circumstances. He drank periodically, going on a spree for from one to three weeks, and then totally abstaining for six months or more. Twice I treated him for the disorders following acute alcoholism, mostly disorders of the nervous system, once for incipient delirium tremens. About six months preceding the attack which terminated fatally, and about one month after a characteristic excess, he complained of some heart disturbance. An examination, however, disclosed no organic trouble, but the pulse was rapid, 90 to 100, and feeble. According to instructions, he returned twice more for examination and advice. A noticeable improvement upon his second visit was followed by a complete return to the normal state upon his third visit. The debauch which ended in his death was like many that had preceded it excepting that it had not continued so long, being voluntarily cut short by the patient himself because of extreme palpitation of the heart. For four or five days after the withdrawal of the alcohol he ate but little, was weak and cyanosed, and had a feeble pulse running from 98 to 130 per minute. About eleven o'clock on the morning of the sixth day of abstinence, while sitting on the edge of his bed in the act of putting on his shoes he fell over, and expired in a few moments.

Post-mortem examination was held twenty-four hours after death. There was some irritation of the mucous membrane of the intestinal tract with a few petechial spots near the cardiac end of the stomach. The heart showed no organic change beyond what might be considered a lack of normal firmness of its muscle. An examination of the brain was not permitted.

Of the three other cases in which death could apparently be traced to direct exhaustion of the heart by the irritant action of alcohol, one was a periodic drinker who died suddenly forty-eight hours after the ingestion of the last alcohol, one was a chronic alcoholic who died soon after an attack of excessive palpitation without organic trouble that could be detected by examination, and the third, a moderate drinker with periodical excess, died on the first day of an attack of pneumonia, presumably of heart exhaustion. Of this group the first two were under forty and the last one 52 years of age.

Undoubtedly the usual cause of death from heart disease in subjects of chronic alcoholism is some organic change produced by the long continued action of the poison. Fatty degeneration and dilatation with consequent valvular insufficiency probably are the usual changes; but, in the absence of any of these, direct heart exhaustion must be regarded as the cause of a fatal issue. The lack of nutrition is also an important element in contributing to this species of heart failure. Drunkards, especially periodic drunkards, in their excesses rarely take even a moderate amount of nourishment. Sometimes they will go for days or a week practically without food. With some, too, alcohol produces a species of mania, during which very little sleep is taken. This lack of food, lack of rest, and all the destructive disturbances incident to the ingestion of large quantities of alcohol must contribute powerfully to the fatal issue of heart exhaustion of alcoholism.

Parkes and Wollowicz, in their classical work on alcohol, called attention to the fact that four ounces of alcohol ingested in the course of twenty-four hours causes an additional labor, on the part of the heart, of 12,960 pulsations; and they express the opinion that so much additional labor on the part of the heart, amounting to about one-eighth of the normal work, must speedily lead to exhaustion of that organ. This view, however, is untenable. Mere stimulation of the heart leads to hypertrophy of the muscle which may be compensatory as when the circulation is obstructed, or necessary to meet the requirements of severe physical labor. In either case the hypertrophy is not pathological but necessary for a new order of things. In other words the heart exhaustion of alcoholism is not the result of an increased amount of work which it is called upon to perform; but to the degenerative changes in the heart muscle, nerves or ganglia brought about by the direct poisonous effects of the alcohol. Hypertrophy of the heart in chronic alcoholism is frequently observed; but it may have arisen from co-existent cirrhosis of the liver and kidneys. Another cause of drunkards cardiac hypertrophy, to which not much attention has been given, results from the increased labor the heart is called upon to perform by reason of the enormous quantity of water which is introduced into the circulation of wine and, especially, beer drinkers. The water in two or three quarts of wine in addition to the usual fluids drunk at meal times must add to the intra-vascular pressure in a marked degree. In beer drunkards, who consume from two to sixteen quarts of beer every twenty-four hours, the labor of the heart in ridding the distended circulatory system of this enormous surplus of fluid, must be sufficient to lead to hypertrophy, or in cases in which the hypertrophy is insufficient to meet the increased demands made upon the heart, dilatation must result. As a matter of fact, enlargement of the heart is very common, according to Struempell, in Bayreuth, Munich, and other beer cities of Germany, an observation confirmed by other German physicians.

But the increased amount of fluid within the circulatory organs is not alone sufficient to produce the changes seen in the hearts of beer drinkers. The excess of carbohydrate food material which a beer drinker takes into his circulation with five or ten quarts of beer cannot be appropriated, but remains in the circulation, increasing the specific gravity of the blood, thus adding another factor to the hindrance of circulation. The increased supply of carbohydrate food aids, moreover, in the production of fatty degeneration which, as we have seen, results from alcohol interfering with the normal evolution of fat digestion and assimilation.

VIII.

Alcoholic Irritation of Other Organs.

If we do not lose sight of the fact that alcohol is an irritant and as such gives rise to conditions identical with those attending an ordinary inflammation, we shall find it easy to understand the destructive changes produced in the various tissues by long contact with alcohol. Wherever it comes it produces a dilatation of the blood vessels and an outwandering of the leucocytes. These are finally organized into connective tissue to take the place of the more highly organized tissue which it displaces, or, by contraction, deprives the normal tissue of its proper supply of blood, thereby causing it to atrophy.

In the kidney alcoholic irritation is manifested by an increase in the elements of its cortical substance at first, followed by contraction and decrease in the bulk of the entire organ. The uriniferous tubes are destroyed partly by this subsequent contraction, but chiefly by the direct action of alcohol upon the epithelial cells themselves. The longer the poisonous influence of the alcohol is exerted over the organ, the more likely will be the kidney to exhibit cortical change; but the greater the quantity of alcohol consumed, other things being equal, the more the epithelium is likely to suffer. Another form of alcoholic nephritis has been pointed out by Strumpell, the so-called acute nephritis of alcoholism, in which there is a sudden breaking down of great areas of epithelium. This seems to result from a cumulative effect of chronic alcoholic intoxication.

In the liver and probably in the spleen and pancreas, although not much attention seems to have been given these latter organs in alcoholism, there is an increase in connective tissue of the cortical substance with a destruction of the epithelial cells. In the liver the interlobular connective tissue contract, giving rise to prominences on its surface, characteristic of alcoholic inflammation, a condition known as "hob-nail" liver.

IX.

The Effects of Alcohol on the Nerve Tissue.

Of all tissues of the body those which enter into the structure of the nervous system are the most profoundly affected by alcohol. Here, as elsewhere, alcoholic degeneration is characterized by two classes of changes: A destruction of cell protoplasm and an increase in connective tissue elements; but, as has been shown by Gaule of Zurich, those cells which are the most highly differentiated, which are called upon to perform the most complex functions, suffer the most and are the earliest to be affected, brain and other nerve cells are more profoundly injured than those of any other part of the body.

This destruction of the cell protoplasm is shown in the shrunken, flattened convolutions of the brain of an alcoholic subject, and a microscopic examination discloses an atrophy not only of the cells but also of the nerve fibers. There is a great proportional increase in connective tissue, and a part of the cell atrophy may be due to consequent pressure by the connective tissue upon the cells. According to Bevan Lewis (Text-book of Mental Diseases, 1889,) the vessels which pass into the brain cortex are enlarged, and their coats in an advanced state of inflammatory and fatty change. There is a proliferation of the adventitious sheath nuclei, the protoplasm of which is undergoing fatty degeneration. A great number of scavenger cells pervades the external region of the peripheral zone of the cortex lying immediately behind the pia, "their branching processes forming a dense matting which converts the outermost fourth into a closely netted substance of minute meshes." These scavenger cells are in greatest number where the vessels pass downward through the cortical layers, resembling the connective tissue increase along Glisson's capsule in alcoholic inflammation of the liver. The deepest layer of cells in the brain cortex are the most affected, the upper, beyond the fifth, are sometimes apparently not invaded. The motor area is that chiefly involved. In the lowest layer, the spindle-cell formation, the scavenger cells are sometimes so great in number as to conceal the spindle-cells from view, the nerve elements being preyed upon by the scavengers. In the spinal cord there are similar changes, but particularly in the walls of the blood vessels, some of the smallest vessels being entirely occluded by the increase in their muscular walls.

In recent years much has been done in working out the characteristic nerve changes of acute and chronic alcoholism. The researches of Jackimoff (Bulletin of Anthropology, Paris, 1890,) showed in puppies and dogs which had for a long time been fed on diluted alcohol, characteristic changes. In animals which died of intoxication the brain was congested and infiltrated with new connective tissue cells. The cells of the grey matter of the spinal cord, especially of the anterior cornua, showed intense disintegration, exhibiting many vacuoles, granules and indistinct nuclei. These changes were found also in the medulla oblongata but in a less degree.

Berkley in a paper entitled "The Action of Ethyl Alcohol on the Cortical Nerve Cells" (American Journal of Insanity, July, 1895, and the Glasgow Medical Journal, Dec., 1895,) records the results of the examination of five rabbits which had been fed with dilute alcohol for periods

THE EFFECTS OF ALCOHOL ON NERVE TISSUE. 93

varying from six months to a year, and which had nearly all died in convulsions. In the vascular wall there were only slight changes, principally a slight increase in the nuclei of the intermediary vessels, some thickening of the walls, some crystals of haematoidin in the surrounding lymph spaces, with a definite dilatation of the lymph spaces surrounding the blood channels and an occasional small hemorrhage due to rupture of a blood vessel. The greatest changes were found in the nucleoli. They were much enlarged, roughened, and spongy with elongated projections from the surface. A large number of the pyramidal cells had tumefactions of varying size on their protoplasmic branches or dendrons. These tumefactions commenced, apparently, on the outer end of the dendron and were accompanied by a disappearance of the latter buds of the dendritic processes. In the cells of Purkinjie of the cerebellum the same alterations but more pronounced were observed. The structure of the axis cylinders was normal. The structures of the neuroglia were also invaded.

From the fact that the arterial changes observed were so insignificant, Dr. Berkley thinks that the changes produced could not be the result of lack of nutrition, but must be charged to the direct irritative action of the alcohol on the cell protoplasm.

The observations of Jackimoff and Berkley are confirmed by other investigations. Recently Hoch (American Journal of Insanity, Vol. LIV., P. 600 et seq.) reported the cell changes in a man recently dead of delirium tremens. These changes he found were uniform. The cell substance which ordinarily takes the stain for observation is lost and that which ordinarily is not susceptible to staining takes the coloring matter instead. The cells have a mottled appearance. The nuclear wall is uncommonly distinct and the nucleus contains numerous sharp granules which are often seen distributed in the net-work. The nucleolus is not enlarged but may show light areas. The next change, a greater disturbance or destruction of the cell, shows the nucleus lighter, the nucleus wall less distinct and more irregular in its outline, the nuclear net-work loses its sharpness and the nucleolus becomes paler and in some instances distinctly smaller. In the last stage the nucleus becomes very pale, either small or very large, often very ragged in its outlines, the nuclear membrane being indicated only by dots, the contents being indistinct and speckled with numerous granules. The nucleolus is either of normal size or very small, very pale, or it may be entirely absent, this being the most common occurrence. These changes are most prominent in the deepest layer (the fifth) and least pronounced in the second layer of cells. The dendritic processes far away from the cell assume a crumbled appearance.

In the neuroglia there are large white spaces around the nuclei, the cell body is visible in parts, often having granules in it, the pigment is often well seen, the chromatin is present in coarser granules than normal, and there is an increase in the neuroglia nuclei. Besides we have in the first layer well marked spider cells.

The vessels frequently present no abnormality, some stand out prominently, partly on account of the neuroglia nuclei of the surrounding tissue. The vessel walls are unaltered.

What chemical changes are undergone during the process of cell degeneration is not known. There can be no doubt, however, that they are as important as the structural changes would seem to indicate.

Commensurate with the physical changes shown by the microscope are the changes in nerve function in all parts of the nervous system. These are first to be noticed in the psychic domain, and the ethical side of the alcoholic's character is the first to exhibit the deterioration. These are almost imperceptible at first and take the form of simple irritability. Trifles annoy him. Petty displeasing incidents which would have passed unnoticed in his normal condition now call forth expressions of anger out of all proportion to the importance of the incident. The alcoholic himself recognizes this unfavorable change in his disposition; but, instead of giving up the drink which causes it, he seeks relief in the narcotism afforded him by increased potations. While in this condition he is apt to regret his impatience. He seeks out those friends to whom his irritability may have given offense and apologizes with profuse and often maudlin volubility.

Later he grows suspicious of those around him, thinks that he is neglected by his friends and that he is not accorded a just measure of gratitude for favors he may have done them, and is liable to attach a great deal of importance to a trifling act of this kind done by him. If his friends notice the change in him and warn him that he is injuring himself with drink, instead of giving due heed to the advice, he is liable to consider this an infringement on his personal liberty, an unwarranted interference with his private affairs, and he will resent it to the extent of putting a friend of a score of years on the list of his enemies.

The moral sense suffers enfeeblement and deterioration. He who was once so punctilious in the matter of meeting his daily obligations becomes evasive and neglectful. That nice discrimination with which he formerly met and promptly attended to the various complicated questions of social and business ethics is lost, and his mind is seen to be of a distinctly coarser fiber.

Sense of dignity, of honor, of moral obligations, of personal conduct, no longer move him as formerly. He thinks only of escaping from them, for the weakened brain cells are no longer capable of attending to such things without infinite labor which the will power of the alcoholic is no longer able to command. The ego becomes prominent, but it is an ego of very inferior order. He talks much of himself—what he is, what he can do, and is anxious to gain the ear of anyone who will listen to his long rambling imbecile narrations of which he is himself always the hero.

Oftentimes the character of the inebriate is so completely the opposite of that of the same man when sober that one marvels at the possibility of both dwelling in the same individual. A man of affairs upon whose shoulders rests the responsibility of successfully directing an invested capital of hundreds of thousands of dollars, does it with an insight and comprehensive grasp of detail worthy the brain of a field marshal. He is an important social factor, too, and his influence is felt along scores of complicated lines of beneficial action. At home he is a loving husband and father, and abroad he is a gentleman of modest unaffected manners so brilliant and genial that it is a pleasure to be in his society. In his personal habits he is strictly correct, and he carries himself with the confident air of one who is a complete master of himself and affairs. Let this same man be drunk on alcohol every day for a year, and the degenerative changes in the brain cells make him a being so much lower in the scale of social evolution that he might be regarded as belonging to another and infinitely lower race of men. He has not only lost his power to direct great business ventures, but he has no desire to do anything of the kind. All of his ambitions are now represented by an intense desire to get sufficient alcohol wherewith to relieve the physical and mental anguish induced by even a short abstinence. Friends have long since been forgotten, and family ties probably broken by neglect or even hatred on the drunkard's part. His conversation is now the maudlin obscenity of the bar-room, and his associates are the fallen men and women who live by the petty crimes committed in theirs, the lowest stratum of any kind of human society. His personal appearance has suffered no less than his character, and his unkempt, neglected, shuffling figure and repulsive expression are a fitting index of the brain degeneration produced by the long contact of its cells with alcohol.

Finally the alcoholic reaches the condition of real insanity. He is emotional in a morbid degree, intensely self-conscious, fault-finding, perverse, intolerable of contradiction, and easily aroused to violent passion. He may, on the other hand, become indifferent to his surroundings, falling into a condition of stupidity from which nothing, for the time, will rouse him, or he may fall into a condition of simple imbecility.

It is a well-known fact that the will power is early and profoundly affected in alcoholism. The subject loses the power to control his own actions and he is willing to be led by very slight influences. Recognizing his duties, he finds it impossible to perform them, impossible to reach and carry out any plan of action requiring vigorous thinking. The indifference with which he regards his daily duties, with an inability to perform them, gives rise to a distaste for all the occupations in which he was formerly engaged.

Last to fail, as a rule, is intellectual power. It may show itself after prolonged excessive indulgence, even after the body is become a wreck. Sometimes it is, in a fitful way, present to the last. Failure of the intellect is generally first observed as a loss in power to quickly grasp an idea, a loss of vivacity, an evidence that all mental processes are performed more slowly and laboriously. The drunkard is indifferent to all social and other questions which give interest to the lives and intercourse of the healthy. His conversation is broken and his ideas fragmentary. Finally the memory fails in a marked degree, and he soon reaches a stage of mental degeneration which renders him unfit for any useful calling.

The above sketch touches only a small part of the phenomena due to the continued use of large quantities of alcohol. Organic changes in the viscera, the digestive tract, liver, heart and other organs complicate in a thousand ways mere nerve degeneration, giving the disease picture an almost kaleidoscopic aspect; moreover, there are hereditary influences at work which are aroused by indulgence in alcohol and contribute their part in modifying the surface play of alcoholic degeneration.

Of disturbances relating to the special senses, hallucinations of sight are common, hallucinations of hearing sometimes present, as are also those of smell and taste. Of sensation, anesthesia or hyperesthesia may be present, as well as abnormal sensations of heat or cold. Amblyopia is common, probably from the degeneration of the cortical cells.

Disturbances of motion in chronic alcoholism is common, and may assume a variety of forms and different grades of severity from slight ataxia with numbness to almost or quite complete paralysis. In my experience the lower limbs are oftener affected than the upper, and the feet the most usual site both of sensation and motion anomalies. The arthrodynia described many years ago (New England Journal of Medicine and Surgery, 1822,) by

James Jackson, is prominent in many cases. The pains are persistent and at times excruciating, accompanied by a feeling of numbness which causes the patient much anxiety. Progressive atrophy of the muscles, especially of the extensors, takes place, causing a contraction of the flexors to such a degree that from this and the paralysis the patient may be entirely crippled. Many other writers have noticed these changes since Jackson wrote of them, notably Lancereaux, Huss, Wilks and Dreschfeld.

A typical but mild case of alcoholic paralysis is now under my care, and I cannot do better than give a complete history of the course of the disease as exhibited in him. This man is now forty years of age, and up to eighteen months ago had been addicted to periodic alcoholic excesses ever since he was seventeen years old. With increasing years his excesses increased until about three years ago, at which time he "took a course" in a commercial institution for inebriates. For a year afterwards he drank no alcoholic liquor excepting an occasional glass of beer. He felt well at this time and attended to his duties as bookkeeper in a lumber yard for several months, and was able to do his work well and without unusual fatigue. He then began to drink large quantities of whisky and brandy, his daily average for a period of seven or eight months being a quart or more. He is able to tell exactly how much he drank, for he bought the liquor by the gallon.

He came under my care, in the present instance, only two months ago; I cannot, therefore, speak accurately of his condition just after he ceased taking this enormous quantity of alcohol. From what he says, however, I judge that his present condition of ataxia or paralysis is as it was at that time only in a less degree. The parts involved are the right knee and foot and to a less degree the right shoulder. He has had almost continuous pain and soreness of the right knee extending down the leg to the foot, associated with a feeling of numbness and formication in sole of the foot. He is troubled a great deal by a sense of insecurity of the affected member. If he happens to step with the heel upon a projecting knot or other prominence in the way, his knee is liable to give way and cause him to fall. The sensation as he describes it is like that one experiences when he attempts to walk when his foot is asleep. The shoulder is not so painful as the knee, and the hand shows none of the anomalies of the foot. The muscles are not apparently atrophied. He complains of uneasiness in the region of the right cerebellar lobe, accompanied by a dull ache; and, when he looks upward, he has a sensation of dizziness and inability to retain his equilibrium, indicating a possible degeneration of a cell area in the cerebellum.

Two other cases similar to this case occurred in my experience a few years ago. In one paralysis was bilateral, almost complete, and affected only the lower extremities. In the other only one lower extremity was affected and here the pain and anesthesia were more prominent than the paralysis. A peculiarity of the first case cited is the long continued persistence of the ataxic symptoms after the alcohol is given up; for in all the other cases which I have observed the withdrawal of the alcohol was attended by rapid progress toward recovery.

Degenerative changes in the peripheral nerve filaments have been described by Leudet, Dreschfeld, Lancereaux, Dejerine and others. Huss was unable to find any changes in the five cases dead of alcoholic paralysis.

Where the peripheral nerve filaments suffer degenerative changes it is difficult to say how much is due to direct alcoholic irritation and how much to lack of nutrition. The recent researches of Hoch (Loc. Cit.) showed that while the nerve cell might be profoundly degenerated the axis cylinder was apparently unchanged. Reasoning from this, we might conclude that the peripheral nerves may not be directly affected by alcohol.

The evil effects of alcohol upon the rapidly developing tissue cells of the entire organism in childhood deserve special attention. Here, protoplasm activity, as is the case in embryonic tissue and the nervous tissue of the adult, invites alcoholic destruction; therefore small quantities of the poison have a relatively greater influence than upon the organism of the adult.

Excepting among the most vicious classes in the overcrowded tenement districts in our large centers of population, the stronger alcoholic liquors are seldom given to children as a beverage. Among foreign born parents, however, a not inconsiderable quantity of alcohol in the form of beer and wine is daily given to children from a few months of age upwards.

As a remedy, however, the ever present brandy bottle has been a panacea in the ordinary household for all kinds of slight digestive troubles incident to childhood, even children in the cradle having a little lime-water and brandy put in their nursing bottles to correct "acidity" and give strength to the little victim of mal-nutrition. This form of domestic medication, having the authority of medical books and medical men, may go on for weeks and months, and the seemingly small daily quantity may do an incalculable amount of harm to the already weakened tissues of the tiny patient. Demme cites (Einfluss des Alkohols auf den Organismus des Kindes, P. 48, et seq.) two cases of real alcoholic sclerosis of the liver in boys, four and a half and eight years of age respectively, the first of which was given whisky for colic, and the latter received it as a stimulating tonic. Both cases, of course, terminated fatally. Many cases of lack of mental development from the same cause, are mentioned by the same author; and of particular interest are several cases of epilepsy, typical in all respects, the origin of which could be directly traced to the poisonous influence of alcohol upon the impressionable tissues of childhood. Cases of epileptic attacks, eclampsia, chorea, and many other nervous disturbances, mild and severe, directly resulting from the exhibition of alcohol in the early years of life, might be cited.

Other writers in recent years have raised a warning voice against the administration of alcohol to children, and especially against allowing them to drink any kind of alcoholic beverage. Professor Nothnagel (Verhandlungen des VII. Congresses fur innere Medicin, Wiesbaden, 1888, P. 137,) characterized the giving of wine at the table to children of three or four years of age as "a cancer of our age."

X.

The Influence of Alcohol Upon Embryonic Tissue and Heredity.

The action of alcohol upon the rapidly growing cells of the embryo is undoubtedly more destructive than upon mature tissue, if we are permitted to reason from analogy. It is easy to understand that the protoplasm of cells which display great activity, even if that activity is only vegetative in character, must be in a condition of great physiological irritability, needing only a comparatively weak stimulus to push it beyond the limits of normal activity to cell destruction. We may compare the irritant action of alcohol with the ordinary irritation seen in inflammatory processes, in which irritation may be only sufficient to stimulate an increase in new tissue, or the process may be so energetic that the tissue is broken down, as is seen in the ordinary process of suppuration. The embryonic cell already possessing a high degree of the same irritability which results from all inflammatory processes, it needs only a comparatively small amount of stimulation to accomplish its destruction. Moreover, the narcotic effects of alcohol must play an important part in hindering the normal course of the biochemical processes necessary to physiological cell integrity.

In the work of Dr. Wilkins (Loc. Cit.) the administration of alcohol was supplemented by fifty-one postmortem examinations, from which he concludes that the cell walls enclosing the germinal matter are dissolved, the albumen not in combination coagulated, the red blood corpuscles are deprived of their constituents, which mingle with the liquor sanguinis, leaving them shrunken and wrinkled, and the organizing ability of the protoplasm is modified. The result is to fill up the connective spaces with foreign compounds favoring the growth of tumors and neoplasms. Chemical selective power is either impaired or completely destroyed, rendering wounds difficult to heal. Two conditions cause this. In the first place, although there is an abundant proliferation of pure germinal matter, it cannot be organized because of the degeneration above mentioned, but proceeds to further degeneration into pus cells because of the continued irritation. Secondly, metabolic life is suspended because the ganglions are deprived of phosphorus and protagon by the direct solvent action of alcohol. Thus the neurodynamia in the grey matter is not properly organized, the enlarged soft parts disintegrate and neoplasm forms in the wounds, while the broken bones receive no osteoblasts to repair damage.

Fere reported a series of very interesting experiments (Journal of Anatomy and Physiology, Paris, March and April, 1895,) in which he undertook to demonstrate the effects of direct contact with alcohol with the bird embryo. For this purpose he dosed a number of hens' eggs with small quantities of alcohol before placing them in position for incubation. Several living chickens were hatched out at the end of twenty-one days, but the most of them were not ready, at the end of that time, to leave the shell because of insufficient development, a large yolk being still retained. Some were killed by the alcohol, and those which were not could not leave the shell before the twenty-third day. Of peculiar interest was the fact that many of the young birds presented various anomalies and monstrosities, such as deficiencies of the abdominal wall, double terminal phalanges and nails, crossed beaks and the like. One of the birds was an epileptic and all might be regarded as alcoholic degenerates.

Fere's experiments also show that alcohol vapors arrest the development of the embyro in the egg of the fowl, and he believes that these results prove that the same obtains in the case of alcoholism in the human subject.

That the progeny of lower animals show the degenerating effects of alcoholic parents is a matter which is engaging the attention of some experimental physiologists at the present time. Of great interest in this connection are the experiments conducted by Professor C. F. Hodge of Clark University. The subjects of his experiments were two pairs of Cocker spaniels, healthy and of the same age, the males being brothers and the females sisters of distantly related parentage. One pair received a daily supply of alcohol, but not sufficient in quantity to noticeably intoxicate. The other pair received the same kind and quantity of food but no alcohol. Nine litters of puppies were born to each pair, those of alcoholic parentage numbering 20 and those of non-alcoholic parentage 16. Of those born of the alcoholized parents 6 were born dead and 8 had some sort of malformation, only 4 being healthy. To the non-alcoholic parents 1 was born dead, and only 1 was malformed, the remaining 15 being perfectly healthy. In other words, only 20% of the progeny of the alcoholized parents were healthy, while 93.8% of the progeny of the non-alcoholic parents were healthy in all respects. This result agrees very closely with the results of Demme's ten alcoholic and ten sober families.

Reasoning from the destructive influences of alcohol upon protoplasm in general and upon the extremely active protoplasm of the embryo particularly, we are prepared to understand the evils which may be transmitted by the alcoholic parent to his offspring, long ago recognized by observing medical men. So many observations of this kind have been made that anything like a complete record of them would consume much more space than may be given to that subject in this work. More than twenty-five years ago Alexander Bain, the psychologist, expressed a belief, as the result of evidence he was able to collect, that no child conceived while either parent was in a condition of alcoholic intoxication could be perfectly sound mentally and physically. This is, no doubt, an extreme view, for we must admit the force of modifying circumstances, such as other hereditary influences in the parents aside from alcoholism, the amount of damage done to the tissues at the time conception took place, and whether both parents were alcoholic habitues. In short, the actual amount of damage done to parental tissue as a whole by the continued use of alcohol ought to be an index of the amount of deviation from the normal standard of health exhibited by the child. It ought not to be forgotten that the heritage of alcoholic degeneracy usually descends through only one parent, the father; the mother, in America at least, being almost always free from acquired alcoholic taint. There should be, therefore, in cases in which the mother is sober and herself free from hereditary taint some chance of producing normal, healthy progeny. As a matter of fact, instances of the kind are common in the experience of every one who has taken the trouble to make the necessary observations and investigations. Many instances might be recalled of strong, sound, forceful, mature young men and women who are the sons and daughters of drunken fathers. As to whether alcoholic degeneracy may leave the next generation unmolested and reappear in the second or third, no definite observations, so far as I am aware, have yet been made. The difficulties attending the collection of statistics of this nature are necessarily so many and so great that no valuable conclusion could be arrived at.

Wilson of Kansas City (New York Medical Journal, Sept. 22, 1894,) thinks that if conception takes place at the time when one or both parents are in a condition of alcoholic intoxication or have been in that state for a time sufficient to cause a deficiency in the nerve centers there will be a corresponding deficiency in the child. Not that all the children of alcoholics are weak-minded or idiots; but, when the conditions exist as stated above, a weak mind or idiocy is the result.

Haushalter of Nancy gives an interesting case of alcoholic degeneracy exhibited in the offspring of a chronic drunkard (Revue Medical, Paris, July 10, 1894). The father is forty years old and shows all the outward signs of an excessive habitual consumer of alcohol. The mother of about the same age looks worn and many years older; she, however, never had any specific disease. The first male child was born dead. The fourth, seven and a half years old, was brought to the hospital in a wretched state. Although fully developed, strong, and robust at birth, he is now pale, emaciated, and with a dry scaly skin. The child is addicted to vicious habits, silent, morose, and terrified, crying upon the slightest occasion. Haushalter expressed his belief that the deplorable moral and physical degeneration is due to the fact that the child is "the last born of an alcoholic father."

Personally I have come in contact with many cases of inherited degeneracy from an alcoholic father as striking as this cited by Haushalter. Space will permit a description of only a few and I select four families well known to me as fairly representative cases of inherited alcoholic degeneracy.

First family: Father a drunkard for twelve years. No hereditary taint in father as far as could be ascertained. Two sisters and one brother sober and useful members of society. Drank to excess from time of his marriage until fourth child was born excepting an interval of about two years. Cessation of drink during this period was due to removal into an isolated settlement where intoxicating drinks could not be procured without much difficulty.

First child female, well developed and healthy in early childhood. Later became nervous and anaemic and had two attacks of chorea before puberty. With appearance of puberty asthma developed accompanied with various psychic disturbances, periodical nervous excitement, hysteria and melancholia.

Second child, male, was a typical degenerate mentally. Given to attacks of violent passion and rage, cruel to animals and children whose weakness made it safe for him to bully them, intractable at home and at school, with the appearance of manhood he committed some punishable offense and was obliged to seek safety in flight, from which time he passed from under my observation. So far as I know he was not addicted to alcoholic drink at the time of his escape.

Third child, female, still born.

Fourth child, male, fairly well developed and in good health. When last seen he was seventeen years of age and his steadygoing habits were often the subject of remark by his degenerate elder brother. It is interesting to note that this child was born less than six months after his father again began his alcoholic excesses, which terminated fatally in three years.

The fifth child, born two years after the fourth and while the father was in a condition bordering on alcoholic imbecility, was an interesting study. He was under observation from the time he was eight years of age until his fifteenth year. As a child he was well nourished and healthy in appearance, but walked with the uncertain gait of a mildly choreic subject. This incoordination affected the muscles of the upper extremities, though in a less degree, and the child's speech was halting and stammering. At school he was timid, lacking self-confidence in his classes and seeking the constant companionship and protection of his more robust elder brother. He learned rapidly and was very faithful to his school work; with increasing years the incoordinated movements became less marked, possibly from greater efforts to control them, but when last seen they were still to be noticed, especially when he was excited.

Second family: Father and mother of good heredity, have seven children. The first four, born while the father was sober and prosperous, are in good health and have had no disease except the ordinary diseases of childhood. After the birth of the fourth child the father became a drunkard, since which time three children have been born, not one of which exhibits the strength of any of the first four. All are nervous, have nutritive disturbances, and the youngest exhibits signs of hydrocephalus.

Third family: Father a drunkard, heredity unknown, has no alcoholic excesses, but drinks a small quantity of beer occasionally. Mother at the time of her marriage to present husband had one healthy female child. Two children resulted from the second union, both male; one appears to be in a normal condition of health, but the younger one is idiotic and has recently been sent to a home for the feeble-minded.

Fourth family: Heredity of mother unknown, heredity of father good. Mother's habits good, but father has been a drunkard ever since his marriage and before. Two children have been born to them, both of whom exhibit trophic disturbances in a marked degree. The elder child is one of the most restless and irritable I have ever seen, and exhibits frequent excessive emotional storms, is of poor color, emaciated, sleeps poorly, and in many other ways shows profound nervous disturbance. The other child is a victim of mal-nutrition amounting to marasmus, and has been beset by adenoid vegetations of naso-pharynx and larynx which twice rapidly reappeared after their removal from the pharynx. So conspicuous were the trophic changes in the case that a colleague discussed with me the probability of an existing specific taint, but we could find absolutely no evidence to warrant that conclusion.

That there is an hereditary alcoholic degeneracy manifested by an abnormal desire for alcoholic drink without serious physical or mental disturbances seems to be supported by good evidence. A case in point is that of a prominent and intelligent man of affairs, under my care at various times for alcoholic excesses, who finally died of alcoholic cirrhosis of the liver. He gave a very detailed account of the alcoholic family of which he was a member, for three generations. His paternal grandparents were both drunkards and all his paternal uncles and aunts, with the exception of one of the latter, drank to excess. In his immediate family, the father and two brothers were drunkards, while a brother and a sister only were sober. He declared to me also that his little children, girls six and nine years old respectively, at that time, had already exhibited the consuming desire for strong drink which had characterized so many members of his family. He described his own desire for drink as absolutely uncontrollable. His excesses were periodic at first, and when the desire seized him absolutely nothing but the fact that to secure drink was a physical impossibility would prevent him from satisfying his morbid appetite.

Another case of transmitted morbid appetite without other disturbance mental or physical was that of a young man whose mother drank large quantities of brandy during his intra-uterine life. This woman was of good parentage and surroundings and had never taken any alcoholic drink of any importance until her first pregnancy. At this time her desire for alcohol assumed the form of a morbid longing characteristic of her condition. Her husband was absorbed by his business affairs and she was left to gratify her morbid appetite at will. This she did until her son was born, after which she had no further desire for alcohol. Excepting an indefinite history of "nervousness" the boy exhibited no abnormal tendencies until the age of puberty was reached. At this time he evinced an intense liking for all kinds of liquors, and in early manhod became a confirmed sot. When last seen by me he had reached a condition of idiocy, and I learned of his death soon afterward.

Of statistical evidence showing the blighting effects of alcoholism in the parents upon the offspring, that recently reported by Legrain is most instructive (Medical Press and Circular, London, Jan. 13, 1894). This report includes vital statistics of 215 alcoholic families represented by 819 descendants. Of this number 16 were born dead, 37 were born prematurely, there were 121 premature deaths, generally attended by convulsions, 55 cases of tuberculosis, 38 cases of marked physical debility, and 145 cases of mental derangement. Of the remainder, "a large number were epileptics, hysterics, idots, etc." These observations were made in France and the author attributes the rapid depopulation of that country to the great increase in alcohol consumption, or, rather, he considers this as of prime importance as a cause of the depopulation of France. Hitherto the French have been regarded as a sober people, but they deserve that reputation no longer, for in 1892 they consumed nearly 40,000,000 gallons of alcohol. In 1789 France was the most thickly populated country in Europe, representing 27 per cent. of the entire European inhabitants. To-day she represents only 12 per cent., the excessive death rate being infantile. During the ten years preceding 1894, 42,000 children were still-born and 240,000 children between the ages of one and five have died annually. Apart from other causes contributing to this result, great prominence is, by general consent, given to alcohol. This has been occasioned largely by the increasing manufacture of wine charged with impure alcohol.

Legrain emphasizes the fact that drunkenness is a fertile cause of unhealthy issue. The simple condition of drunkenness at the time of conception is sufficient to cause mental and physical inferiority in the offspring. This degeneration in the children of alcoholics may result even though neither parent may be actually under the influence of alcohol at the time of procreation.

Forel is convinced that chronic alcohol poisoning in the parents is transmitted to the offspring in the form of various mental and physical anomalies (Medical Pioneer, Endfield, Eng., Nov., 1893). The heritage may descend in the form of an irresistible craving for alcohol, physical debasement, mental disease, idiocy, and a multitude of other disturbances. Hereditary craving for alcoholic drink may exist when neither parent drank from any other motive than that of sociability. He found, too, that these abnormal descendants bear alcoholic liquors badly and are easily intoxicated.

Vigillis of Italy (ibid.), discussing the heritage of criminals, says that 32 per cent. of all criminals have criminal tendencies as a direct inheritance from their parents, and that alcoholism in the ancestry is a most fruitful cause of criminal tendencies. Corre of the French military service (Quarterly Journal of Inebriety, Jan., 1894,) believes that 40 per cent. of crime and reprehensible conduct comes from inherited alcoholic degeneration from inebriate parents.

C. H. Hughes of St. Louis (Alienist and Neurologist, Jan., 1894,) recalls Morel's table of alcoholic neuropathic degeneration extending through four generations as follows:

FIRST GENERATION: Immorality, alcoholic excesses, brutal degradation.

SECOND GENERATION: Hereditary drunkenness, maniacal attacks, and general paralysis.

THIRD GENERATION: Sobriety, hypochondria, lypemia, maniacal attacks, and general paralysis.

FOURTH GENERATION: Feeble intelligence, stupidity, first attacks of mania at sixteen, transmission of complete idiocy, and probably extinction of family.

More recently Legrain presented in the British Medical Journal a great many observations which, when tabulated, lead him to draw the following conclusions:

(1) Double parental alcoholism creates an irresistible tendency to drinking in children.

(2) Parental absinthe drinking seems to directly transmit epilepsy to the offspring.

(3) Parental combination of absinthe drinking and epilepsy is a common cause of epilepsy in children.

Fuerer of Heidelberg (Bulletin Medical, Paris, Aug. 25, 1895,) expresses the doctrine that the generative cells of the drunkard are alcoholized and that the offspring are, for that reason, frequently degenerates: psychopathics, idiots, or rachitics. He makes a distinction between those cases in which there is only an inherited desire for drink and those in which there is some inherited organic fault. He admits, however, that one form may coexist with or engender the other, both being the result of real degeneration. He thinks it absurd to think that an evolutionary adaptation of the human kind to alcohol will ever be brought about, insuring it immunity against alcoholic poisoning. Facts prove the contrary. The intoxication of the male and female germs weakens the resisting force against alcohol in the descendants instead of strengthening it. It is impossible for an evolutionary adaptation to narcotic poisons to take place.

Speaking of the influence of alcoholism in producing degenerative offspring, Crothers (Journal of American Medical Association, April 9, 1898.) remarks that heredity has in these cases left the person a low and defective vitality, feeble powers of resistance, and inability to adjust himself to his surroundings. These conditions of weakness and degeneration diminish the power of resistance against inflammatory disease, and also make narcotism by alcohol fascinating because the subject thus acquires a feeling of strength and his physical and mental distress are at the same time relieved and deadened; moreover, the families of inebriates and consumptives are often very numerous. Where the degradation of the parents is unmistakable, the number of children is often very large, confirming the oft noted fact that just before extinction of the race a supreme effort is made to perpetuate the seed and save it from obliteration. While the inebriate families are often large, they die young. If they live through childhood, they carry with them into maturity defects which soon cause their extinction. Several cases illustrating this are cited. Two degenerate members of a famous family in New York united, both of whom were moderate drinkers. Thirteen children were born, five of whom died in infancy, and eight reached the age of maturity. Three of this number were drunkards and died of tuberculosis, one died of acute pneumonia, one became demented, and two died with some low fever associated with rheumatism. The one still living has been eccentric and feeble-minded all his life. Not one of the descendants of these people is living. Of another family, three of the nine members came for treatment for inebriety, one relapsed and became insane, the second was killed by accident, the third is a low drunkard. Two of the remaining children died of tuberculosis, one is an eccentric reformer with extreme zeal, but little wisdom, and one is a paranoiac single woman. The parents were healthy drinking people, without business, who died in middle life of some acute disease.

Degenerate families of this kind are by no means uncommon, especially in older sections of the country. They appear in the two extremes of great fecundity or barrenness. When a general history shows that the family is degenerating, growing weaker in appearance and conduct retrograding, tuberculosis and inebriety with hysteria, eccentricity, rheumatism, and a variety of nerve diseases are almost sure to follow. Members of such families are sometimes brilliant and precocious. A son of one of these dying families took high honors at college and entered upon a brilliant professional career, in which he became eminent; but two years later he became an inebriate and died of tuberculosis. His inherited degeneration had been masked by his display of vigor and precocious brilliancy.

Baer has pointed out that in sections of the country given to excessive drink there is a smaller percentage of young men fit for military duty than is to be found in those parts in which the people are temperate, and Gyllenskiold says that since the full benefit derived from the recently enacted laws regulating the sale of intoxicants in Sweden has become apparent, there is a smaller number unfit for military service because of physical weakness and low stature, than before these laws were enacted.

In an address delivered in 1874 by the Director of the Council of the Canton of Bern in regard to the management of a model distillery, the evil done by this institution was described in the following words: "In our Canton, without any difference in age or sex, the consumers of spirits have so largely increased that it furnishes an explanation as to why the large, strong, fresh, fine figures are becoming more rare, why the recruit transports contain so many small, bent, prematurely old individuals with expressionless, yellow, stupid faces, and why the number of acquired and not congenital nervous diseases is increasing." (From Demme's Einfluss des Alkohols auf den Organismus des Kindes, Pp. 35 and 36.).

In Demme's comparison of ten families of drunkards with ten families whose members were temperate their life histories disclosed the following facts: Of the ten drunken families there were 57 direct descendants. 25 of these died in their first year of insufficient vitality, 6 were idiots, 5 were dwarfs, 5 epileptics, 1 choreic and idiotic, and 5 had hydrocephalus, hare-lip, and club foot. Two of the young men were epileptic and had inherited alcoholism. Only 17.5 per cent. had ordinary good health in childhood. Of the temperate families there were 61 direct descendants. Only 5 died in infancy of congenital lack of vitality, four had curable nervous diseases, and two more had some congenital defect. 81.5 per cent. were mentally and physically sound in childhood and youth.

XI.

Alcohol as a Factor in the Production of Insanity.

From the evidence cited above the conviction that alcohol is an important causative factor in the production of insanity cannot be avoided. It is extremely difficult, however, in the vast majority of individual cases, to determine exactly how much of the disturbance may be charged to alcohol, either directly or indirectly, and how much to other causes near or remote. In order to reach anything like a correct conclusion, a history of the direct and collateral family ties of each person, for at least three generations, would be absolutely necessary, and this should be supplemented by a minute personal history from infancy until the onset of the mental disturbance. While the latter may sometimes be approximately or quite complete, the former is rarely or never complete enough to be of definite value for the purpose of fixing alcoholic responsibility. Furthermore, recognizing the difficulty of obtaining such ancestory statistics, superintendents of hospitals for the insane have probably paid little attention to the matter, and there are available no records of even the small number of cases the histories of which might have been obtained with a valuable degree of completeness.

One of the foremost statisticians in the United States (Dr. Frederick Wines) writes me that he has no statistics on the subject; and those he has seen were not trustworthy. Another writes me that he is now collecting evidence of this kind, but that it will be many months before it is analyzed. From a letter received from a third I quote the following paragraph: "We have very little literature on the subject. During the last year in this institution there were 409 admissions. Fifty-four cases were recorded as intemperate. There were probably 15 cases in which this was not given as a cause that I personally know to have been intemperate, and I have no doubt that there are others in which the use of alcohol was an etiological feature and was not set forth in the examination papers" (Dr. W. A. Gordon, Northern Hospital for the Insane, Wis.). In letters from several other superintendents of insane hospitals, no statistics of the kind are available. Of course the mere fact that an insane person had been addicted to alcohol in excessive quantities is of small importance in determining the cause of his insanity unless he could prove a good inheritance and sound health up to the time of his alcoholic excesses; for, as we have seen, alcoholism may be an effect as well as a cause of central nervous disturbance.

A committee is now engaged in collecting statistics upon alcoholism and insanity, but statistical evidence of this kind is of slow growth, and many years must elapse before it can assume a definiteness and proportion sufficient to make it of value. The most complete statistics on the subject of alcoholism are those collected by the authority of the state of Massachusetts for the year ending with August 1st, 1895 (Twenty-sixth Annual Report of the Bureau of Statistics of Labor). There were confined in state institutions for the insane 1,836 persons, 974 of whom were males and 862 females. In point of age, only 78 were under twenty years. The decade having the greatest number was that between thirty and forty,

ALCOHOL IN THE PRODUCTION OF INSANITY. 119

there being 457 of that period. The next greatest number occurred between twenty and thirty—405, while 372 occurred between the ages of forty and fifty, 235 being fifty and sixty, 254 between sixty and eighty, while only 30 were beyond eighty years of age.

Of the whole number of insane (1836) 311 were said to be excessive drinkers before the occurrence of insanity, 360 were moderate drinkers, while 677 were total abstainers. The habits of the remaining 488 with regard to alcoholic indulgence could not be ascertained. It will be seen, therefore, that 16.94 per cent. of the insane were excessive drinkers, 19.6 per cent. were moderate drinkers, and 35.87 per cent. were total abstainers, while from 26.58 per cent. of the whole number no information upon this point could be obtained.

Subtracting those cases of whom no information could be obtained regarding habits of alcoholic indulgence, there remained 1,348 whose habits were known, 699 of whom were males and 649 females. Of these known cases, 35.48 per cent. of the males were excessive drinkers and 26.32 were total abstainers; while of the females 10.02 per cent. were excessive drinkers and 75.96 per cent. total abstainers.

Information regarding the habits of the parents as to indulgence in alcoholic beverages could not be obtained in 939 or 51.14 per cent. of the cases. In 616 cases, comprising 316 males and 300 females, one or both parents were intemperate, while in 281 cases, 128 males and 153 females, one or both parents were total abstainers.

As to whether the inmates' insanity was directly due to the excessive use of alcoholic beverages, in 330 instances no information could be obtained. Of the remainder, in 383 cases, including 296 males and 97 females, replies were obtained showing that insanity was directly due to alcoholic excess. In 1,123 cases, including 479 males and 644 females, the insanity was said not to be due to excessive alcohol consumption. Therefore, expressed in percentages, the point as to whether the lunatic was made insane by alcoholic poisoning was not ascertained in 17.97 per cent of the cases; insanity *was* the result of alcoholic poisoning in 20.86 per cent. of the cases, and it was *not* the result in 61.77 per cent. of the cases.

Going into the question as to whether the intemperate habits of one or both parents led to the insanity of the lunatic, produced the following results: In 1895 cases no information could be obtained, in 20 cases the reply was "yes," and in 921 cases the reply was "no," that is, no information could be obtained in 48.75 per cent. of the cases, the negative replies were 50.16 per cent., and the affirmative replies 1.09 per cent. of the whole number, 6 of which were males and 14 females. In 184 cases insanity was attributed to intemperate habits in the grandparents, in 170 cases the grandparents were said to be temperate, and in the remainder of the cases, 1,482, no information regarding the habits of the grandparents in this respect could be ascertained.

This question was also asked: "Did the intemperate habits of others (neither parents nor grandparents) lead to the insanity of the person considered?" In 123 cases the reply was "yes," in 757 it was "no," and in 956 cases no information could be elicited.

Analyzing the above statistics, it will be seen that of the whole number of insane patients whose habits could be learned 35.48 per cent. of the males and 10.02 per cent. of the females were excessive drinkers. But excessive drinking might not have been the cause of the insanity, it might rather be the result of some neurosis. Further on, however, we learn that out of a total of 1,506 cases alcohol was held to be the direct cause of the insanity in 383 cases, 296 of which were males and 87 females. As had already been stated, the habits of only 699 males as to their indulgence in alcohol could be learned, and 296 attributed their insanity to alcohol directly. Thus we have 42.5 per cent. of all the males whose habits in this respect could be ascertained made insane by alcoholic poisoning. Of the 649 females whose habits in this respect are known only 87, or 10.86 per cent., were made insane by direct alcoholic poisoning.

Of the evidence which these statistics contain, that relating to heredity shows that 1.09 per cent. of those from whom information on the point could be obtained attributed their insanity to parental intemperance, and 123, or 6 per cent. of all concerning whom grandparental influence could be ascertained attributed their insanity to that cause.

Taking for granted that the cases concerning which the direct or ancestral influence of alcohol could not be ascertained would show the same percentages as those in which it was ascertained, we would have a total of probably about 45 per cent. of all the cases of insanity in this group chargeable either directly or indirectly to alcohol. This method of drawing conclusions, however, should not be permitted.

A further fault of the above statistics is the fact that many of the cases may have been influenced in several ways by alcohol, directly, through parental or grandparental or collateral relatives' intemperance. All such cases would be counted in each class, and be considered as not one insane patient but as many as there are classes. Statistics of this kind are not valuable.

Insanity statistics in the United States are not reliable. The census report for 1880, for instance, showed the following number of insane person for every 100,000 inhabitants: Foreign white 398.8, native white 161.9, and negroes 91.2 respectively, while the census report for 1890 showed 387.0 foreign white, 140.5 native white, and 88.6 colored insane to each 100,000 inhabitants. The total number of insane reported for 1880 was 91,959, while the total number of insane reported in the census returns of 1890 was 106,485, showing that in the decade the number of insane persons increased a trifle more than 15 per cent. But the population increased 24 per cent. in the same time. In 1896, however, the National Conference of Charities and Corrections reported 145,000 insane persons in the United States, an increase of nearly 37 per cent. in six years. The only conclusion to be drawn is that the statistics of the United States census reports are of no value in showing whether insanity has increased or decreased. It is generally believed, however, that insanity is increasing, and this increase is shown in statistics for localities. Whether insanity is increasing in the same ratio as the per capita consumption of alcohol we have no means of knowing.

Something more definite regarding this matter has been obtained in Europe. In the German Empire alone in 1877 there were 4,272 patients undergoing treatment for alcoholic insanity in public institutions. In 1885 this number has increased to 10,360, an increase out of all proportion to the increase in population (Die Gefahren des Alkoholgenusses, Dr. Servus).

According to the statistics of Baer there were, in the years 1878 and 1879, 4,013 male lunatics in the German insane asylums, the insanity of 1,088, or 27 per cent., of whom could be traced directly to the influence of alcohol. Of these 690 suffered with delirium tremens. If we reckon with these the patients who were treated in private institutions, the total of alcoholic insane amounts to 2,016 yearly. Furthermore, in the years 1878 and 1879, the yearly number of patients suffering from the extremest forms of alcoholic disease in institutions the statistics of which were open to inspection, amounted to 5,212. In those years there died from alcoholic poisoning 1,993 persons yearly. In the year 1885 there were 11,974 such patients in Germany, with a correspondingly high mortality. Considering, again, the Swiss statistics, it was found that of the 366 deaths from alcohol occurring in 1891, 187 belonged to the laboring classes, and 179 were men in the easier circumstances of life.

Of special interest is the fact that the increase in the number of lunatics in the asylums of Germany was very rapid after the middle of the present century, at which time the manufacture of whisky from potatoes was begun. In France also were the effects of this new industry very apparent. In the Bicetre, according to Baer, from 1806 to 1811, the number of male lunatics whose insanity could be ascribed to alcohol was only 11.7 per cent. of the whole number. In 1855 it had slightly increased, but still was only 12.78 per cent., but in 1865 it had increased to the astonishing figure of 25.24 per cent. of the whole number.

In Charanton the proportion of alcoholic lunatics from 1826 to 1835, according to Esquirol, was 8 per cent.; Lagerose estimated the proportion at 24 per cent. in 1857, and by Marsaing it was estimated to average 27.87 per cent. during 1865 and 1870.

In Austria, according to the best of evidence, since the beginning of the fiftieth year of this century there has been an average yearly increase of 2 per cent. in cases of insanity, and these increasing recruits are said by Gauster to come exclusively from the ranks of alcohol drinkers. What this increase means will be better understood when it is known that every ten years a new asylum capable of accommodating 600 patients must be erected, and that 2,000 more apply each year for treatment than applied forty years ago. At the time when this report was obtained about 40 per cent. of all the cases of insanity affecting males could be ascribed to alcoholic excesses.

Recent statistics upon this point in Germany are not accessible. The last obtainable showed that 27 per cent. of the male and 3.2 per cent. of the female lunacy patients became such through excessive alcohol consumption. In institutions which lie near large centers of population the percentage of alcoholic insane is considerably greater. Statistics from Prussia especially show a rapid increase in the number of insane. In 1852 to 1854 there were only 3,631, but the number had increased to 8,481 in 1870 to 1872, an increase out of all proportion to the increase in population.

"In another place I have already stated what seems to me of the utmost importance, that we in Germany are so universally accustomed to look upon alcoholism as the normal condition, the basis, in a certain degree, of the normal physiological man, that our physicians need the strongest kind of hint (with many, even an attack of delirium tremens is not sufficient) to lead them to the thought that the illness is the result of chronic alcohol poisoning" (Dr. August Smith, Die Alkoholfrage, P. 74).*

*"In anderem Orte, habe Ich erwaehnt, was mir zu wiederholen wichtig scheint, das wir in Deutschland im allgemeinen so sehr gewoehnt sind, den chronischen Alkoholismus als Normalzustand, die Grundlage gewissermassen des physiologischen Menschen anzusehen, das es bei unseren Aerzten schon der aller kraeftigsten Hinweise bedarf (ein Delirium Tremens genügt manchen dazu

noch nicht) um bei einer Erkrankung nur den Gedanken einer Alkoholvergiftung aufkommen zu lassen."

Some significant statistics came from the Dalldorf Asylum (Mansfield Holmes in Medical Pioneer, Aug., 1895), where, out of a total of 1,234 patients confined, 450 were children. Rust, the physician in charge of the asylum, considered the large percentage of insane children due to the fact that habitual drinking was the rule and not the exception. Investigations by the local authorities show that alcohol may produce insanity by acting as an exciting cause, or it might produce an hereditary insanity by transmitted debasement in children in the form of predisposition. Rust thinks periodical excessive drinking more likely to produce insanity in the subject himself, but that habitual constant drinking is more apt to breed hereditary insanity in the offspring, and that bad heredity as a determining cause of insanity played a most important part with the patients in this institution. H. Piper, one of its physicians, stated that up to 1882, at which time he began his observations, the total number of reliable cases then collected in the German statistics was 1,287; of this number 860, or 66 per cent., were traced to hereditary causes and the balance, 427, or 33 per cent., to acquired causes. This is a proportion of two cases of heredity to one of acquirement. Of 416 cases collected by himself during the twelve years following 1882, 310, or 75 per cent., were traced directly to hereditary causes, and 25 per cent. to acquired causes: a ratio in favor of hereditary causes of three to one.

Undoubtedly, however, many cases of insanity due to alcoholism are the result of children of tender years ingesting large quantities of alcoholic liquors, rather than to inherited tendencies alone. I have seen in the city of Berlin children from five years of age upwards given free quantities of strong wine and beer, the effects of which must have been seriously deleterious; and Moreaux of Tours, France (Annales Medico-psychologiques), considers alcoholism, so prevalent in children, only partly due to hereditary influence. Drunkenness in these cases is sometimes seen at a very early age, and when there is a hereditary predisposition a small amount of alcohol is sufficient to produce intoxication. He found in alcoholic children marked evidence of evil dispositions leading to criminal tendencies. The continental custom of giving young children wine is a powerful factor in bringing about this state of affairs, while some responsibility rests with the indiscriminate prescribing of alcoholic medicines by physicians. He had seen delirium tremens in children four or five years of age, brought about, as in adult life, by the sudden stopping of alcohol with children who were habitual drinkers.

More recently Jakubowitsch (British Medical Journal) reported increasing drunkenness among the children of Russia, where vodka, an acrid drink containing from 40 to 50 per cent. of alcohol, is the national beverage. He also tells of children four or five years of age having had delirium tremens. Parents there, he says, often thoughtlessly give their children spirituous liquors to improve the color of their cheeks, make their eyes sparkle, or induce sleep. He also discusses the influence of alcoholism in the parents in producing hereditary defects in the children, and cites cases similar to those already given in another part of this work in which children begotten while the parents were sober were healthy and intelligent, while others conceived when the same parents were intoxicated showed marked cases of physical and mental degeneration. Among the least progressive peoples of France, especially those of Brittany, children are, at a very tender age, habituated to the daily use of spirits. In Great Britain and in our own country, though in a less degree, in large centers of crowded and vicious population the use of drink among children of a tender age prevails to an alarming extent, and the consequent physical defectiveness and moral degradation lead to habits of viciousness and immorality shocking in the last degree.

It would be no easy task, therefore, in cases of insanity among children due to alcoholism to determine how much of the disturbance may be due to the direct effect of alcohol and how much to hereditary effects where both, as is very frequently the case, operate as determining causes.

XII.

The Attitude of the Medical Profession Toward Alcohol.

About the value of alcoholic beverages in the normal condition of health there is only one medical opinion, and that is that they are entirely unnecessary and therefore do no good. In America at least a small number of physicians would probably express the opinion that "moderate drinking is not harmful," perhaps the same number would hold that any amount of alcohol in health is harmful, while the great majority are probably influenced by their surroundings and have no fixed opinions upon the subject.

As to the value of alcohol in disease, medical opinion is again divided. There are many physicians, and the number is growing, who believe that while alcohol has some value in diseased conditions this value is very limited, and that it performs no duties as a curative agent which could not be better and more safely performed by some other agent. A much larger number, however, especially those who were educated on the continent of Europe, still cling to the traditions of medical practice and prescribe alcoholic beverages in various diseased conditions, especially such as indicated a lowered vitality, lack of appetite and strength. I say this is done as a matter of routine practice, for I believe that the majority of physicians who do this have not given the subject any particular attention, but are bound by the authority of precedent. Among men

THE ATTITUDE OF THE MEDICAL PROFESSION. 129

who have to deal with nervous diseases and with insanity, at least here in America, alcohol as a therapeutic agent has no place.

Certainly no other remedy for the treatment of disease has been as extensively used as alcohol in the form of some alcoholic beverage. Its use received a great impetus about the end of the eighteenth century in England from the teachings of that time, which would see the causes of all diseases in a condition of "sthenia," or "asthenia," according to whether the surface play indicated increased activity of the heart and "plethora" or the lack of them. For the former bleeding, emesis, and catharsis were the prime remedies, while for the latter nothing found so much favor as alcohol.

The first half of the present century was completely under the influence of those teachings. Todd and his pupils treated all inflammatory diseases, especially typhoid fever, with enormous quantities of alcoholic liquor. It was not an unusual thing at this time for a patient ill with typhoid fever to receive two or three bottles of strong red wine, port, or burgundy, besides a considerable quantity of champagne and cognac, as much as a quart of the latter often being given within the course of twenty-four hours.

Todd and his school were followed by the greatest lights of the profession in both Europe and America. Trousseau, Moneret, and Terrier in France advised a free administration of alcohol in typhoid fever. Soulie treated all his cases of typhoid, whether mild or severe, with rum in doses of 60 to 80 grams (Bullet. de Therapeutique, 1870), and Bouvier was conspicuous in his advocacy of the administration of strong wines in typhoid fever. In Germany Liebermeister, Riegel, and Juergensen used large quantities of alcohol in treating typhoid fever and the so-called "asthenic" inflammations of the lungs. Daret and Breisky gave the same treatment for puerperal fever; Leyden, for gangrene of the lung, and Volk, for the treatment of erysipelas. It was held by all of these eminent men that alcohol within proper bounds and where there was no definite contraindication was of the utmost importance in relieving the prostration incident to all of those exhausting diseases, and that during the course of the fevers alcohol would not intoxicate.

European medical opinion was very naturally reflected in America. Here medical writers of twenty-five years ago, or even of a more recent date, almost uniformly advised the administration of alcohol in all inflammatory diseases attended by great exhaustion. There were some prominent dissenters from the generally accepted creed, but they were few in number compared with those who clung to alcohol as a stimulant. Indeed, within the past few years, if a physician were advised to "stimulate" his patient he would take that advice to mean that his patient should receive alcohol in the form of strong spirits. Recent developments in chemistry and biology, especially in the chemistry and biology of bacterial diseases, are forcibly bringing to the notice of the profession the errors of past teachings as to the stimulating value of alcohol.

There are a few medical men who openly espouse the cause of alcohol, not only as a valuable remedy in disease, but as having increased the sum total of human happiness. Some of these men have given reasons for the faith that is in them, while others have been content to merely express their opinions. The number of these men, however, is small compared with those who hold opposing views. It will be instructive to examine the views thus set forth in order to learn the evidence upon which they rest.

Mortimer Granville has said: "Drunkenness is in no other sense the consequence of drinking than the destruction of a house by fire is the consequence of having a cooking range on the premises. The moment appears opportune for a little plain speaking and I trust that this may be permitted in one of those who seeks to convert the public mind—that alcohol in all its forms is needless to the healthy and only of questionable value to the sick—to those who hold that it is far better that the healthy should be moderate drinkers than abstainers, and that the great value of alcohol in the treatment, and I will go farther and say, in the prevention of disease, should be clearly recognized. I am perfectly well aware that in professing this strong belief that abstinence from the use of wine or beer is a worse evil than occasional abuse of these intoxicants—I use this form of expression advisedly —I am placing myself in antagonism to the majority of medical writers on this subject, but I am so thoroughly convinced of the accuracy of this view after years of study and observation of the subject, in its professional and social aspects, that I should be lacking in moral courage if I hesitated to express myself decidedly. I sincerely believe that incalculable harm has been done to the human organism with its functions, which we are wont to classify as mental and physical, by the spread of teetotal views and practices. There is less stamina in the life of the average Englishman now than there was fifty years ago. He may live a little longer, but he is not so well able to resist the invading germs of disease, or to recover from the depleting effects of such invasion, as he was when good wine and sound ale was an integral part of his daily diet. He has lost some, if not much, of the practical advantage due to the diminution of preventable maladies by improved sanitation, because he has allowed his organic life to fall to a grade lower in vital energy than that which previously protected him against perils greater than those that now beset him. Asylum physicians go their rounds and notice that a very large proportion of those who became insane previously drank to excess; but if the bulk of the general practitioners outside of the asylums were asked what proportion of those who habitually drank became insane—which is a very different matter—the evidence that drink plays an important part in the production of insanity would be found to fall to the ground. I doubt whether, of the great bulk of general practitioners who have the opportunity of collecting information upon this subject, any large number could compile twenty cases falling under their individual observation of persons who habitually drank freely and became insane. It is needless to the point to tell us that of insane persons many once drank. We want to know the proportion of persons who drink that is passing into the class of lunatics. So far as I have been able to ascertain, this portion is so small as to be insignificant. Meanwhile, a calm and grave survey of the statistical and facts will show that not a few terrible diseases, such as consumption, cancer, specific maladies of low type—for example, diphtheria, the worst forms of gout, nervous troubles, and a host of minor ailments—have for their cause asthenic conditions of vital force in the organism which render it, as a whole, weak in the presence of its enemies, and, as to its constituent parts, prone to the degradation of organic types of life, and have developed and extended their ravages since the substitution of table waters for the sound (malt and hop and grape) fermented beverages has sprung into fashion at the instance of temperance advocates. These are grave assertions to make, and I am not insensible to the responsibility which attaches to the physician daring to make them; but I am persuaded that the time has come when those who do not share the views it is fashionable to profess ought to declare themselves."

It is not necessary to point out the many errors in the views of the above writer. Here are a group of bold assertions without any evidence to support them, except the casual observations of the writer, not one of which but is abundantly refuted by exact methods of observation and investigation, the results of which have already been fully set forth in this work.

When the attention of the great Charcot was called to Tolstoi's article on alcoholism, he replied (British Medical Journal, July, 1891): "I am compelled to admit that I do not find the article of Tolstoi very able. It is exaggerated, and, therefore, false. Alcohol and tobacco are injurious, but they can be used in moderation. There are numerous examples of this. Moreover, before alcohol and tobacco there came into the world abominable things. Indeed, since their introduction civilization has rather softened. Must one say, then, that alcohol and tobacco are immoral forces? In everything I hate extreme positions. I believe in common sense, and I do not see that the position of Tolstoi conforms to its dictates."

There is always a disposition to attach importance to the opinions of great men without regard to the basis upon which they are founded. The mere fact that some one in authority has promulgated the opinion is sufficient to give it weight without regard to its intrinsic value. Because "civilization has softened" (if there was any civilization before the introduction of alcoholic beverages) since the introduction of alcohol and tobacco, how does that prove the value of these narcotics unless they can be connected as cause and effect? Such methods of reasoning are childish.

Another example of this specious mode of reasoning is found in an article by Dr. S. S. Herrick (Journal of the Am. Med. Assn., Feb. 19, 1898): "This alleged degeneracy has been going on ever since Noah planted the vine and got drunk on its products, on coming out of the ark, yet within the period of profane history the span of human life has doubled and is increasing. France, Spain, and Italy are producing annually, according to different estimates, fifteen to forty gallons of wine per capita, most of which is consumed at home, and this has continued for centuries; the output of wine and beer in Austro-Hungary is about fifteen gallons annually per capita, and in the German Empire double this amount. On the alcoholic basis, degeneracy in the latter progresses twice as fast as in the former. In these European countries children drink fermented liquors from the time they are weaned, and follow the habit all their lives. Inasmuch as human life is steadily lengthening, popular education extending, and military power growing, the present writer fails to see proofs of degeneracy."

Arguments of this kind will convince no logical mind. Why did not Dr. Herrick use his own statistics to draw another conclusion? He has said that the consumption of wine, per capita, in France, Spain, and Italy is nearly three times that of Austro-Hungary, and one and a half times that of the German Empire: therefore, should we not look for a greater amount of degeneracy in the Latin countries than in either Austria or Germany? If this writer really believes in his own method of reasoning, he should have reached the conclusion that the degeneracy of France, Spain, and Italy, recognized by all intelligent people, is really due to their excessive use of alcoholic beverages. He should not have been content to point out that Germany is no more degenerate than Austro-

Hungary, though the former does consume twice as much alcoholic liquor as the latter. As to his statement that the children of these countries "drink fermented liquors from the time they are weaned and follow the habit all their lives," enough has already been said of the deplorable results of this reprehensible habit, yet the statement is made by this writer to carry the impression that no evil results follow. If he fails to see proofs of degeneracy it must be from the fact that he has not examined the evidence. It is absurd to take a few general facts, ignore the rest, and then draw sweeping conclusions. I cannot leave this article of Dr. Herrick's without calling attention to another example of his most fallacious reasoning. He calls attention to the fact that "the native populations of Old and New Mexico, having been subjected to smallpox with little or no modification by vaccination for three and a half centuries, have acquired a great tolerance" and that "the races of tropical America have become tolerant of yellow fever that total immunity is claimed for them by some writers," therefore, we must conclude, people long accustomed to alcohol and other narcotics will also get a degree of immunity which will make alcohol harmless. But alcohol does not and cannot give such immunity. It is so different in its nature from the poisons of small-pox and yellow fever, so different in the biochemic changes which it produces in the body, that any attempt to compare the two indicates an absurd lack of knowledge of immunity processes.

In a comprehensive work on dietetics (Practical Dietetics, W. Gilman Thompson, M. D., 1896,) the subject of alcohol is treated at considerable length. The author excuses a full presentation of the subject upon the plea that it would be too long for the limits of his book, hence we do not know upon what evidence he bases his conclusions, which are as follows: "The problem whether the world as a whole is better or worse for the existence of alcohol, aside from all ethical questions, and viewed merely from a scientific standpoint of the influence of alcohol upon mortality, is difficult of solution; for, to offset the numerous cases of fatal alcoholism and still larger number of cases of diseases which would not presumably be fatal without the existing condition of chronic alcoholic poisoning of the system, are very many cases among both infants and adults in which life is undoubtedly saved by the prompt resort to this food and stimulant and its energetic use. So long as man is exposed to hardships and conditions arising from improper and deficient food supply, as well as the numerous infectious diseases to which he is heir, alcohol must still be regarded as a blessing rather than a curse; for there is no form of stimulant and food combined, or stimulant alone, which, taken all in all, can be so completely relied upon in cases of emergency. Alcohol when taken alone will prolong life beyond the period at which it terminates from starvation."

From the above conclusions one who has knowledge of all the evidence must wholly dissent. They are in direct opposition to the great mass of experimental truths which have resulted from the most laborious, painstaking, and exact methods known to science, and which have been fully discussed in this work. There can be no hesitancy in making a choice between the loose generalizations and guesses founded upon unsupported statements, and the knowledge actually gained by experimental research.

There is still another class of physicians who for clinical reasons alone have discarded alcohol as a therapeutic agent. These are busy, practical men, good observers and quick to take advantage of any remedy, the value of which is apparent, without taking the time to inquire very closely into the reasons for the good results exhibited. These men, I find, are almost a unit against the giving of alcohol in diseased conditions excepting where the patient happens to be an alcoholic habitue and its withdrawal would be attended by serious nervous disturbances.

One physician of this class, who has enjoyed a large general practice for more than twenty-five years, in answer to my question, declared that he had not prescribed an alcoholic beverage for more than ten years, and his reason was that he had never observed any good to result therefrom. A surgeon who is a teacher of anatomy, and who also is surgeon of a railway company, in which capacity he has to deal with many acute injuries attended by pain, loss of blood, and shock, answered the same question by saying that he not only did not use alcohol in dealing with these cases, but neglected no occasion to caution the railway employes against taking spirits in case of their own injury or giving it to their fellows under the same conditions. His observations had led him to believe that nervous disturbances were prolonged and intensified in those cases in which alcohol had been freely given, which was often done before he could reach the patient. A physician of ripe age and many years experience with hundreds of old men in a Soldiers' National Home said that alcohol is the worst enemy of the veterans under his charge. Not only do the majority of fatal issues resulting from some inflammatory diseases take place immediately after an alcoholic excess, but he has seen no diseased condition improve under the administration of spirits in either small or large quantities. The men who totally abstain are better nourished, freer from disease, and carry their years more lightly than those who take alcohol in any quantity. Many of the inmates are alcoholic inebriates. They demand their accustomed drink and get it. It is possible that some of these would die sooner if it were suddenly withdrawn, therefore, in these cases, alcohol probably prolongs life. Nearly all of this class have organic diseases directly traceable to the long continued use of alcohol.

XIII.
Who Become Drunkards and Why?

That the great majority of drunkards become such through the influence of social environment cannot for a moment be doubted. To drink and ask the companionship of others in drinking alcoholic beverages is the first lesson in the primary school that develops the confirmed drunkard, and to drink and ask others to drink is and always has been so much an integral part of social functions of a large part of our people that time and observance have elected them to the position of at least quasi-social duties. The ease with which intoxicating drinks may be obtained wherever there is any considerable aggregation of people makes the practice of this social custom quite universal. It would be absurd to deny that the social status of indulgence in alcoholic beverages does more to make drunkards than all the other causes combined, for the sanest of individuals, beginning to drink through the influences of social environment, may become as hopeless a drunkard as any defective member of society. So subtle are the processes of the narcotics, of which alcohol is one, in creating a need on the part of the nervous system for a repetition of the same drug, that the habitue becomes such before he is aware; and his chance to regain his former mental and physical condition, other things being equal, is in exact ratio to the amount of damage he has sustained from alcoholic poisoning.

To show how great is the influence of social drinking

in the production of drunkards one has only to recall the fact that the vast majority of drunkards are of the male sex. Here in America, where the drinking of alcoholic intoxicants does not prevail among the women as a whole, the ratio of male to female drunkards is certainly as great as one hundred to one, and probably much greater. Assuming that heredity is as influential in producing female as male alcoholic degenerates, which, according to laws of heredity, must be true, the preponderance of male drunkards over those of the female sex must be attributed to the increased opportunity for alcoholic indulgence enjoyed by the male. Nor can there be any reasonable doubt that many male defectives, the victims of a neuropathic heritage from alcoholism or any other parental cause, would become useful and reasonably happy members of society could their enforced abstinence from alcohol be assured, but these are almost always the unfortunate victims of social drinking. The pleasing effects of alcoholic narcotism once experienced, the habit of alcoholic excess is soon formed; and the will power, always insufficient, is still further weakened until resistance is no longer possible and the degenerate abandons himself to the bestiality of satisfying his vicious appetite.

XIV.

What Is Inebriety?

The term inebriety is rather loosely used, both by the profession and by the laity. In its simple and broader sense it means no more than habitual intoxication. Formerly it meant merely the condition of drunkenness; now it is by common consent applied to those cases which exhibit an overmastering appetite for narcotics in quantity sufficient to intoxicate, together with the gratification of that appetite. When unqualified, alcoholic inebriety is understood. Dr. Norman Kerr has suggested that "inebriety" be displaced by the term "narcomania," which he defines as "a mania for intoxication by an intoxicant." This gives the term a new aspect, for, according to this definition, a narcomaniac would be an inebriate whether he indulged his abnormal appetite or not.

Inebriety is called a disease, and the term is modified to suit the special narcotic for which the subject evinces an abnormal appetite. There may, from this point of view, be as many forms of inebriety as there are narcotic drugs capable of producing their forms of intoxication. There is a general belief, upon the part of the laity at least, that the inebriate appetite is selective from the beginning, that certain individuals evince an overmastering desire for certain narcotic drugs and that they will be satisfied each only by a particular narcotic. Especially does this view prevail with the public as to alcoholic inebriety, and certain influences which will be discussed later have done much to spread and confirm this view.

In former times drunkenness was considered as always a voluntary and vicious act, and punishment was meted out of various degrees of severity, from fines and imprisonment to whipping, torture, and death. Indeed, a visit to a police court in any of our larger municipalities on any of the working days of the year will convince the observer that, though the whipping post, the pillory, and the scaffold have been abolished nothing better than fine and imprisonment has yet been discovered as a corrective for public drunkenness. In more recent years, as a result of medical investigation, there has grown up a belief that the drunkard is not always responsible for his acts, that he may be physically and mentally defective, and that he should be treated, not as an offender against the law, but as a sick man who is afflicted with a species of insanity. The public, or at least that part of the public philanthropically inclined, has seized this idea; but, not possessing that discriminating power which is possessed by medical men, have come to regard all drunkards as afflicted with that disease called inebriety, and to think that "its victims are irresponsible." This idea is erroneous and mischievous, but it has been so persistently fostered and so widely disseminated by certain commercial institutions that its teachings have had an enormous effect. It is not sufficient to say that medical men know that this teaching is false. The mehods adopted by these institutions have made it the most prominent factor in the alcohol question in America during the past eight or ten years, and its influence has been many times that of thoughtful medical men who have stood for the truth. These institutions teach that inebriety is a specific disease. We need not discuss the purposes for which they do so, when we call attention to the fact that a specific cure is offered to all who can afford to pay the price. Neither is it necessary to call attention to the various sophistries set forth by its supporters to bolster up this syndicated opinion, for the purpose of refuting them. We must not forget, however, in our practical dealings with the alcohol question that the "literary" machinery of this venal institution has probably converted a majority of the laity to its views.

The statement that inebriety is a disease should not be taken without qualifications. It is generic rather than specific. It is no more a disease than nervousness or dropsy. It is a morbid condition of the nervous system which craves the intoxicating effects of narcotics. This craving may arise from degenerate conditions resulting directly from the action of the narcotic upon the subject himself, it may come to him as a congenial fault, or it may be the outgrowth of nervous disturbances coming on at any time of life from any cause. In short, anything which makes existence continuously painful tends to produce inebriety by driving the victim to such means as may be most easily available to find relief. There are many examples of a selective appetite manifested in early life, a preference exhibited for a particular form of narcotic, but this appetite very rarely or never becomes evident until the subject has actually experienced the intoxicating effects of the drug of his choice. To show that this is true one has only to recall that alcoholic inebriety very largely preponderates over all other kinds, and that the number of male inebriates is very much in excess of the female. This is due to the fact that the habit of drinking and treating prevails almost exclusively among males, thus giving every opportunity of arousing any latent defect, or, rather, of suggesting that alcohol be drunk because it is seen to contribute to the apparent wellbeing of the drinker, who may be the victim of a latent defect. On the other hand, such occasion for bringing out latent defects does not often come to the female. If they exist they are more likely to be disclosed by the physician's prescription. For this reason, while as alcoholic inebriety among women of respectable standing and habits is very rare, other drug addiction is much more common. Morphine, chloral, bromides, and, more rarely, cocaine habitues are in my experience much more common among the latter than among the former, and their inherent morbidity was almost always aroused, in the first instance, by something prescribed by the family physician. There can scarcely be any doubt that opium inebriety would be the most common form prevailing if preparations of opium pleasing to the taste were sold under the same conditions which now regulate the sale of alcoholic beverages.

It should be understood, then, that inebriety instead of being a specific disease which always drives its victim to some form of narcotic excess is simply a defect in his nervous organization which makes his condition, his existence, under the influence of some narcotic intoxication more pleasurable or less painful than during abstinence.

Inebriety arising from nervous defects presents many variations of type and widely differing degrees both of nervous disturbances and excesses in alcoholic indulgence. It may be periodical or continuous.

XV.

Intermittent or Periodical Inebriety.

Men, especially young men, who are occasional drinkers sometimes drink to excess. It would be difficult to find one of this class who has not at least once felt the intoxicating effects of alcohol. To some a single experience of the painful after effects of alcoholic poisoning is sufficient to prevent a repeated indulgence, but the number is not large. Here again social influences predominate to make the occasional drunkard. There is an undefined, and generally unspoken sentiment, among boys and young men that a physical tolerance for alcohol is an evidence of mature manhood; and, therefore, that he who is able to drink the greatest amount of the intoxicant at hand without showing signs of complete intoxication is deserving of respect. To have a "weak head" for wine is to invite derision and reproach. In stories of England's country gentlemen, they have been described as "two bottle," "four bottle," or some other number of bottles, men, meaning that they habitually drank that number of bottles of wine, generally port wine, after dinner, and to be a "twelve bottle man" was to excite no little admiration in the rural community. Similarly on the continent of Europe, and especially in Germany, is this sort of manly superiority recognized at the present day. There, as is well known, the students of various universities have their beer drinking contests for the purpose of electing a "beer king," the last man or boy to "fall under the table" from sheer acute alcoholic poisoning being unanimously chosen to wear the royal ermine of King Gambrinus.

The idea that social superiority attaches to an ability to drink large quantities of alcoholic beverage exists in a still more marked degree with the lower orders of society, while a "weak head" is assailed with a deeper measure of contempt. I have heard many stories of this sort of prowess among the lumbermen of the north, mill hands, and lake sailors, while I have seen poor weaklings intoxicated with whisky furnished by their more accomplished fellows in order to be made the butt of rough ridicule. I have known a periodic drunkard to drain an ordinary table tumbler full of raw whisky at a single draught before sitting down to his breakfast, turn to a companion, and say, "Ah, Joe, me boy you will be a dandy when you can do that!" and I have known of a "boss" in a lumber camp who refused to hire a man because "he could stand so little whisky."

The influence of this sort of public opinion in the production of inebriety cannot be overlooked. Not only is it calculated to rouse all the latent desire for narcotic intoxication, but it may drive the novice, even though it cost him several painful experiences, as is the case in acquiring the tobacco habit, to acquire not only a taste, but an imperative need, on the part of his abused and degenerated nervous system, for alcoholic narcotism.

There may, therefore, be many occasional or periodical drunkards whose excesses are caused by certain determining influences without the existence of any inherent defect. To apply the term inebriate to these would be to confuse the subject. They are, as far as may be ascertained by any method of examination, mentally and physically sound before and after their alcoholic excesses.

A smaller number of periodical drunkards are true degenerates. Without apparent external cause, in the face of promises and protests to the contrary, against the prayers of those who have the greatest influence over him, and in the face of impending business ruin and personal disgrace, alcoholic excesses are begun and continued until the storm has exhausted itself in a debauch. Then comes a period of deep remorse sometimes leading to suicide. Always there is deep contrition, renewed earnest promises of reform, and a sincere and often successful attempt to repair the damage done to health and character, a period of successful decorous life, and again a sudden plunge into alcoholic excesses. "Many men who fall into persistent drunkenness are unaware of their neuropathic heritage of unsteady nervous organism bequeathed to them through alcoholic or other depressing influences operating in their ancestors. Not understanding the tyranny of their unstable system, they censure themselves as fools for each bout of drinking, resolving and re-resolving not to do it again, and then go on and do the same unless aided by medical art to overcome the tyranny of the degenerated organism" (C. H. Hughes in Alienist and Neurologist, Jan., 1894).

Several marked cases of this class of inebriate have been under my care or observation at various times. Nearly all belonged to alcoholic families. One I treated several times for incipient delirium tremens. Twice during periods of remorse following protracted debauches, while consulting me in my office, the unfortunate man fell upon his knees and with tears streaming from his eyes and hand uplifted, against my protest, made a most solemn oath never again to drink another drop of alcoholic liquor. Scarcely two months after his last interview with me, I saw him again in the beginning of another drinking bout. He was active, noisy, irritable, grandiloquent, arrogant, and proud. He took it as a serious personal affront when I drew him aside to remind him of the danger of his condition, declaring that he was quite competent to take care of himself without any outside interference. This man had large business interests and possessed more than an average amount of intelligence and business capacity. He was of distinct alcoholic heredity.

Another case was that of a fairly intelligent man who had periodical attacks of great restlessness, attended by dizziness, slight mental confusion, headache, and sleeplessness. At the same time an intense desire for liquor possessed him, and he drank excessively for one or two weeks, then. suddenly stopped and resumed his daily avocation, which was a minor judicial office. Unlike most inebriates, he consulted me during a sober interval. He fully appreciated his condition, and described it minutely and intelligently. The periods occurred independently of any surrounding circumstances, and varied in frequency from six or eight weeks to three months. The attacks began with mild disturbances, but increased in severity until he was compelled to seek relief in alcohol. He was advised to keep on hand a mixture of chloral, potassium bromide, and tincture of capsicum, and to take it in quantity sufficient to allay his nervousness as soon as it appeared. He was also advised to remain at home for a day or more, to avoid being irritated by the petty annoyances of his office. This simple expedient kept him from alcohol for more than two years. At the end of that time he lapsed once more into his old habit, but the debauch was not severe, and he declared he made it voluntarily to celebrate a local political victory. He was under observation for nearly a year after this, but no knowledge of any further backsliding came to me.

Three brothers of this inebriate were known to be drunkards. One of them, however, was a successful business man, who, though he drank at times, still possessed sufficient self-control to prevent his excesses from becoming very conspicuous. Another brother has been a drunkard for many years. He drinks continuously and indulges frequently in conspicuous excesses. The third brother was a typical alcoholic degenerate of the periodic type. I attended him through an attack of alcoholic mania characterized by violence, delusions of persecution, and destructive tendencies —homicidal, suicidal, and property. Immediately after recovering from this maniacal attack, when the normal functions were all re-established, he escaped from his room during the absence of his attendant, and returned in a few hours in a maudlin condition of intoxication. He was then locked in a cell and kept until his desire for alcoholic liquor could be controlled.

The time elapsing between any two successive narcotic debauches varies much with different inebriates and at different times with the same inebriate. In some the nervous tension is always at the same level and needs only the occasion, the presence of favorable circumstances, to insure a narcotic excess. A commercial traveller who had his work arranged so that he would visit a certain town once in three months, and afterward once in six months. Here he had to wait a week before resuming his travels. He invariably seized this occasion for a drinking bout, four times a year when occasion permitted it, but only twice a year when the old order of things had been changed. Here, it would seem, the periodicity was determined by the periodicity of his visit to this particular town.

Examples of this kind are numerous. Many inebriates

are controlled by the presence of a wife, a mother, or a sister, but the absence or death of the relative removes the restraining force under which the degenerate may have fretted and silently protested, and he at once plunges into the excesses toward which he was so long inclined. Periodicity may, therefore, be determined by the periodicity of occurrence of favorable circumstances and have the same variations.

Another kind of periodicity is that which seems to be the result of accumulated nervous irritation. It is as though a successive train of electrical impulses were sent into a Leyden jar, which finally becomes charged and is, electrically speaking, in a condition of unstable equilibrium, exploding when it becomes surcharged. An inebriate of this kind has tolerably regular intervals of drunkenness, for, no matter what the surroundings may be, to drink is inevitable.

Still another type is epileptic in character. There may be long intervals of perfectly sane decorous conduct, without nervous perturbation of any kind, when the subject is taken by storm and seeks immediate relief in alcoholic or other narcotic intoxication. This type is sometimes seen in women, coinciding with the menstrual function. I have seen a marked example of it in a clergyman's wife who invariably became drunk on port wine with the recurrence of each menstrual period.

By far the greater number of periodic inebriates, however, are those of unstable mental equilibrium, in a constant state of mental depression and irritation, who suffer from ennui, tedium vitae, whose intercourse with the world is fatiguing, who find no joy in occupation, who are given to introspection, and who find their very existence painful. Losses of any kind, in business or of friends, or anything else which may add to the burden imposed by existing degenerate conditions, may make that burden too painful to be borne, and relief is sought in the nerve deadening effects of narcotic drugs, chiefly in alcohol.

Many cases of periodic inebriety are difficult of classification. Certain susceptible individuals seem to be markedly affected by atmospheric conditions. Heat, cold, moisture, electrical tension and the like, may develop a latent desire for drink which would have otherwise remained dormant. In certain other cases there seems to be absolutely no cause for occasional bouts of drunkenness but the pleasure of gratifying the physical taste for some form of alcoholic drink. Drunkards of this kind often have their debauches in solitude and consume only a special brand of spirits or wine. Their periods of excess are, in some cases, at least, far apart. For example, there is the case of a well-known professional man who once a year drank large quantities of a certain brand of whisky. Preparations were always deliberately entered into, a local druggist being asked to have on hand a stated amount of the intoxicant for the occasion, which always took the form of a fishing excursion lasting from one to two weeks. His only companion was a trusted man-servant. During the remainder of the year he abstained from alcoholic beverages absolutely. Another example was that of a wealthy and venerable philanthropist who, every summer, engaged a suite of rooms in a prominent hotel of a distant city, and in the seclusion of his apartments drank enormous quantities of a particular brand of champagne. Ten or twelve days thus spent sufficed to satisfy him for the whole year. Perhaps we may regard these cases as we would cases of simple gluttony, excesses to gratify a momentary taste, without any craving on the part of the nervous system.

XVI.

Non-Intermitting or Constant Inebriety.

The periodic inebriate or the occasional drunkard may become the constant inebriate. Sometimes inebriety is constant from the beginning, but this is not common. The same causes which produce the one form produce the other. In the writer's experience, the sound man of good heritage who acquires the habit of drinking is more likely to become a constant than a periodic inebriate. He creates the necessity for narcotic sedation by his excesses. Some drunkards daily take a sufficient quantity of alcohol to produce a certain state or degree of intoxication for months at a time, exhibit no periods of irregular conduct, attend to their daily duties with the utmost regularity, and finally die of some acute inflammation or some chronic disease engendered by alcoholic irritation. Many of this class have no history of degeneration of any kind. They become the victims of favorable opportunity. They are men of means and leisure, without definite aims in life, to whom normal existence has become dull. Employment may also favor constant drinking. The wine merchant becomes a constant inebriate from drinking his wares with his many customers. So does the distiller and his salesmen; but more particularly do the laborers engaged in the manufacture of alcoholic liquors become drunkards. It is the habit of employes in such places to have a definite amount of the beverage manufactured set apart for each individual daily. The laborer is very jealous of his "rights" in this respect and I have heard of a strike threatened because of a suggestion on the part of a brewer to reduce this daily allowance of beer. The amount allowed to each workman is probably always sufficient to keep him in a continual state of intoxication. I have it on good authority that some brewers of Germany allow each workman eight liters of beer for his individual consumption (a liter is 2.113 pints). Estimating beer to contain from three to eight per cent. of alcohol, the amount of alcohol consumed daily by each man would be from one to two and two-thirds pints. Whether this custom is universal in America, I cannot say. It is observed, at least, in some breweries, but whether it is observed or not the brewery employe is pretty sure to keep himself saturated with alcohol and exhibit its damaging consequences. A medical friend who has considerable practice among these men declared that many of them "are walking pathological museums."

Similarly, bartenders, porters, and other servants employed where intoxicating liquors are sold, readily acquire the habit of continuous excessive drinking, without the existence of any abnormal appetite for drink, but simply because the drink is easily accessible.

Very liable to lead to constant inebriety is the habit of keeping late hours combined with the drinking of alcoholic liquor in quantity to produce slight intoxication. Indulged in, night after night, as is often the case with young men of the store, the bank, or the lawyer's office, they find that the day's work must begin with an aching brain and exhausted body, which may be temporarily relieved by a "bracer" of brandy. When exhaustion thus produced becomes marked, a repetition of the dose at frequent intervals during the day may become imperative to enable the debauchee to do his work, and the way is soon paved to continuous inebriety.

There is a general but ill defined opinion that the continuous inebriate, unlike the periodic inebriate who is the victim of an insane impulse, is somehow personally responsible for his drunkenness, and there is some foundation for this opinion. It is not that the voluntary inebriate, if the expression can be allowed, does not become a degenerate and does not suffer from the withdrawal of his habitual narcotic, but that he began his habit of drink a free man, unhampered by any resistless impulse bequeathed to him by degenerate parents or acquired by other means than alcohol.

As a corollary to the fact that habit alone, without preexisting degeneracy, may lead to continuous inebriety. is the fact that this sort of inebriate is most readily reformed or cured. If great and permanent damage has not been suffered by any important organ, and he is intelligently supported during the nerve storm, following the withdrawal of alcohol, until he has regained his usual standard of health, he is certainly not so liable to lapse into his old habits as he would be if he had some congenital fault to deal with. Here, again, blame should attach to him should he, after complete recovery, again form habits which would lead to inebriety.

The amount of damage done by alcohol which may be repaired by patient and judicious treatment cannot be definitely stated. It is not uncommon to meet with cases of complete recovery after evidence of most profound nerve degeneration—partial paralysis, incoordination, paresthesia, anesthesia, hyperesthesia, marked disturbances of the special senses, and the like. Physicians who have had considerable experience with drunkards will readily recall examples of this kind.

One such case under my observation for a time exhibited signs of most marked degeneration. The muscular

NON-INTERMITTING OR CONSTANT INEBRIETY. 155

system was atrophied, he suffered intense pain and incoordination in the lower extremities, complete anasthesia of one foot, and amaurosis to such an extent that he could not read, nor even oversee the work of his employees (he was a master plumber). A complete withdrawal of alcoholic liquor was followed by prompt improvement, and within eighteen months he had apparently reached his normal condition of health. Nearly seven years have since elapsed, but there has been no recurrence of his old habit.

Not only under intelligent medical handling may inebriates of this class recover, but they sometimes exhibit a surprising amount of will power and enter almost singlehanded into the struggle against the bestiality to which they have sunk. Generally the determination to reform is the result of some profound impression, fear of speedy death if the habit is continued, a religious revival, a disaster to family or friends for which the drunkard thinks he is to blame, or the dying request of a neglected wife or mother.

A "homesteader" in a pine forest of northern Wisconsin, whose nearest neighbor was several miles away, left his wife, who was about to be confined, to call a physician in a village about ten miles away. On arriving he found that the physician was absent and would not return before two or three hours. He then went to a saloon, of which he had for a long time been a liberal patron, to get his jug filled and await the doctor's arrival. Here alcohol soon made him oblivious of his urgent errand, and not until the next day did he return to his home, where he found both his wife and baby dead. The calamity was sufficient to make him abjure alcohol for sixteen years.

A young man of good heritage became a constant inebriate through social influences alone. For a period of eight or nine years he had not been free from alcoholic intoxication for a single day. At the end of this time he had become unfit for any kind of labor. He had the usual symptoms of nerve degeneration, with marked psychic disturbances. For these he called his physician, and asked an opinion as to whether his condition was dangerous to life. He was candidly told that he might die in a short time, and that he certainly would die within two years if he continued his course. With only a very little help from his physician he fought out the battle, and at the end of four or five weeks he could enjoy a normal existence without any narcotic. Eight years have elapsed without a revival of his old habit.

The history of another young man under the writer's observation is almost identical with the above. The latter, however, drank more alcohol and showed profound nerve degeneration, especially of sight. Fear of losing this important sense started him on the road to reform. He, however, accomplished the result quite singlehanded, rejecting proffered medical aid. His cure has persisted up to the present, a period of more than five years. A wealthy lumberman had been a drunkard from the age of eighteen. For many years he habitually became intoxicated on Saturday afternoon and continued so until Monday or Tuesday morning. Besides this he drank more or less during the remainder of the week. Four or five years previous to his reformation he became a continuous drunkard, being under the influence of alcohol during his entire waking time. He ceased drinking at the age of forty-one, giving as his reason the fact that his wife had never upbraided him for his excesses, and that her christian fortitude, together with an overwhelming sense of the wrong he had done her, compelled him to attempt to reform, even though the effort should kill him.

Many other instances of partially or wholly voluntary

reformation might be recalled, but cases of this kind are already familiar to both laymen and medical men. When a considerable number of them are analyzed, it is difficult to escape the conviction that much drunkenness is really voluntary.

Here is an appropriate place to point out more fully some facts, the failure on the part of the public to understand which, have made imposition by commercial inebriate institutions possible. These people send out broadcast unqualified assurances that they "cure inebriety," assuming, of course, that it is a definite specific disease. Many guarantee to "cure" it in from four to six weeeks. Their clients are instructed and assured that this method of cure absolutely abolishes all desire for alcoholic liquors. Not only this, but the former appetite for strong drink is replaced by deep-rooted and permanent abhorrence for alcoholic intoxicants. Their proposition may be stated thus: "You have had the specific disease called inebriety. You are now cured. Instead of having an appetite for alcohol, you now have and always will have an aversion, unless you again begin to drink voluntarily. Should you again begin to drink alcoholic beverages, you will again get the disease of which you have been cured." It is unnecessary to point out the puerility of such arguments. I have known a young man just returned from an institution which promulgates this doctrine declare to a group of old convivial friends that even the smell of liquor nauseated him, and that he felt sure that he not only would never but could never again drink spirits, and then die as the result of a drunken debauch four months later. I attended a man for delirium tremens resulting from a debauch which began the second day after he left this institution, cured, as he was told. A patient under treatment at the present time for syphilis was cured of inebriety in six weeks. A few months afterward he began his old excesses and for a year or more drank more than ever before taking the cure. He then ceased voluntarily, and for two years has been trying to repair his shattered fortunes. A friend upon whose word the utmost reliance may be placed told that he was an eye witness to the following incident: A train bearing several returning "cured" inebriates to a certain city in the west stopped for a time at a way station. Here the returning prodigals met an equal number of the unregenerate on their way to the institution the former had just left; good-fellowship overcame all restrictions and the "cured" and "uncured" got drunk together.

Many inebriates return to those institutions again and again. A brilliant scholar known to the writer is now undergoing his sixth or seventh "cure." Many others are known to have been treated by the same method two, three, four, five, or more times. A few do not fall from grace after taking the treatment once. If a record were kept of all the inebriates thus treated for a period of five years after being discharged as cured, the number which had not relapsed would be found to be very small. In the experience of the writer and, as far as can be learned, that of other physicians, those permanently benefited are almost invariably constant inebriates who become such, not through any inherited or other defect of the nervous organization, but through the habit of social drinking; inebriates of the periodic type, the victims of a true degeneracy, are rarely, if ever, benefited even for a short time. This result is precisely what ought to be expected when the subject of inebriety is understood.

XVII.

Popular Fallacies Regarding Common Alcoholic Beverages.

Perhaps three-fourths of the intelligent people of America believe that alcoholic beverages "taken in moderation" are beneficial. A brilliant German woman once said to me, "I use water only to bathe in." She spoke the sentiment of the German people as to the use of water as a beverage, for no German is so poor that he will not spend a few pfennigs for beer to drink with any meal excepting breakfast. The Frenchman, though he has recently become something of a beer drinker and has increased his allowance of spirits, still keeps up the traditions of his ancestors in his devotion to wine. Similarly in other European countries water as a beverage is eschewed by all classes of society, and liquors containing alcohol are almost universally substituted, because they are believed to be more beneficial in promoting and maintaining the health. There is a curious popular belief among the majority of uneducated foreigners that the drinking of water causes bodily weakness by making the blood "thin," and the physician is sometimes asked if this is not true.

Spirituous liquors, whiskey, brandy, gin, rum, and others, containing forty to sixty per cent of alcohol, are popularly believed to be stimulating when taken in small quantities. As the only active principle they contain (excepting gin) is alcohol, their action is the action of alcohol, and whether alcohol is a stimulant or not has already been fully discussed in this work. In the normal man not habituated to the use of narcotic drugs, in spite of the delusive sensation of increased mental and physical power which follows the ingestion of a small drink of spirits, *muscle and nerve capacity is, in the sum total, always lessened.* This has been conclusively proved by Richardson and others through actual experimentation.

There is also a popular belief that these strong beverages contribute to the physical well-being under conditions of fatigue due to excessive physical exercise, especially if the exercise is taken in a cold and wet atmosphere. A habit prevails extensively, among workingmen, of taking a drink of spirits at the close of a hard day's labor, when fatigue is so great as to become painful. Seafaring men, soldiers on a march, sportsmen, and others whose employment makes exposure to the inclemencies of the weather necessary habitually drink spirits to lessen the unpleasantness of exposure and make their necessary tasks easier. Here again we meet with the familiar delusion that narcotism is strength. Undoubtedly the sense of fatigue is lessened or abolished, but the chemical conditions causing the fatigue remain the same as they were before the ingestion of the spirits, the sensory nerve endings having simply been narcotized into a temporary quiet. Morphine or any other narcotic produces percisely the same effects. Perhaps alcohol is the least offensive narcotic under these circumstances, but it is a narcotic nevertheless. If exercise is continued after the irritations of fatigue are temporarily lulled to rest, muscle and nerve wear and tear still continue. They are not abolished simply because they are not felt. A condition of over fatigue thus results, to recover from which requires a long period of rest; therefore nothing is gained, but there is always a loss due to the temporary derangement of the vital functions by the action of the narcotic.

Similarly, while a drink of spirits seems to warm the subject chilled by an unexpected bath in icy waters or a downpour of cold rain, actual investigation by precise methods shows that the bodily temperature is always lowered when a sufficient quantity of alcohol is taken to affect it at all.

The stronger alcoholic beverages are popularly believed to increase the bodily weight, to give *embonpoint* and the color of health. Even some members of the medical profession hold this view. A recent writer (Practical Dietetics, Thompson, P. 207) makes the following peculiar statement of those who use alcohol: "In the condition of health more food is eaten and more force developed than is actually necessary for the body, and there is constantly a reserve supply of energy on hand which may be used for any extraordinary exertion, and hence the constant use of alcohol as a food or stimulant is both unnecessary and unadvisable." An analysis of this confusing statement would seem to make it mean that the habitual taking of alcohol in the form of spirits leads to an exaggerated condition of nutrition by stimulating the appetite so that more food is taken than is needed, and that the surplus is stored up in the form of reserved force. The physiological principles which make this impossible in the normal subject have already been discussed. Suffice it here to say that spirituous liquors such as brandy and whiskey have no more power to increase the weight of the normal man than have sulphuric ether or chloroform, and that when a drunkard is well nourished or fat he does not confine himself to these alcoholic beverages alone, but drinks others containing food substances. The writer has never yet seen a drunkard who drank spirits alone who became fleshy, but the opposite condition of emaciation always prevailed. Says Dr. Norman Kerr on this point (Alcoholism and Drug Habits): "Spirits drinkers as a rule are more shrunken in aspect and often grow thinner the longer they continue their deep potations till, in many cases, they are quite emaciated." As to the rosy color of the spirits drinker's face, that is due to the paralysis of the vessel walls leading to permanent dilatation, especially of the superficial blood vessels of the face.

Spirits are commonly taken by one who feels the necessity of being braced up to meet a mental ordeal or to tide him over a period of mental perturbation from any cause. Here again it is not the stimulant which relieves, but the narcotic, by making the nervous organism less impressionable to irritating influences. Lastly, spirits are very commonly taken to ward off infection in the presence of epidemics of contagious disease. Confidence in the efficacy of strong brandy and whiskey for this purpose is wide spread. No advice of the physician was more common a short time ago than that instructing the throat to be gargled with brandy and small quantities of it to be swallowed to ward off an attack of diphtheria. Blood poisoning from an infected wound was also combated with large doses of strong liquor. To-day the physician can demonstrate that infectious diseases are made more formidable by the giving of spirits, but the laity will be a long time learning this important fact. Especially are malt liquors supposed to be of exceptional value in contributing to the physical well-being of man. Beer and ale are supposed to have an important tonic and food value, while the amount of alcohol they contain is looked upon as harmless. The opinion is expressed on every hand that the drinking of beer should be encouraged, because it tends to produce temperance—the more beer that is drunk, the less spirits will there be drunk. Indeed, it is difficult to appreciate to what extent beer is regarded as one of the prime necessaries of life with the people of some European countries and their American descendants. With some of these people, not to drink beer is to be considered eccentric, and to doubt its wholesomeness and desirability as a beverage is rank heresy, while to publicly oppose it is regarded as a dangerous degree of fanaticism.

Beer is a mixture of alcohol, sugar and dextrine, carbonic acid, the bitter principle and some other constituents of the hop, tannic acid derived from the hop or from vegetable matter used for coloring purposes, and water. The effects of beer are precisely the effects of its constituents if taken separately but simultaneously. The alcohol in beer produces drunkenness just as it does when taken in any other form, and as beer and ale contain from three to twelve per cent of alcohol the amount ingested will depend upon the kind and amount of beer drunk. Four per cent beer may produce unlimited alcoholic intoxication. Massachusetts passed a law in which an intoxicating liquor was defined as one containing four per cent of alcohol or more, but so much drunkenness could be produced by a beer of this strength that the law was afterward amended so as to define an intoxicating liquor as containing alcohol to the extent of one per cent or more. There can be no doubt that many hereditary appetites for alcohol are first aroused by drinking beer.

There is considerable variation in the amount of sugar contained in different malt liquors. If the sugar and dextrine be taken together, as they have the same food value, the amount would be found to vary from two and a half to three per cent or more in the heaviest ales and porters. Excepting the very small amount of proteid matter contained in malt liquors, which is so small that it may be disregarded, sugar alone of all ingredients has a definite food value. There is a popular belief, and it is not confined to the laity exclusively, that malt sugar, which is found in malt liquors, is superior to the ordinary sugar of commerce, in being more easily digested and assimilated. There is, however, no foundation for this assumption. Indeed, physiologists know that all sugars are changed into the ordinary grape sugar of commerce before being finally absorbed and converted into mechanical force. This assumption probably had its origin in the belief that diastase existed with malt sugar and aided the digestion of starch. Diastase, however, is killled by the high temperature of the brewing process.

Sugar is an important and easily assimilated food. Taken in excess of daily need, it is stored up as fat, and to the sugar alone is due the obesity of the beer drinker. In addition to an abundant supply of fat, the beer drinker also develops the ruddy countenance of the spirit drinker, due to the same cause—alcoholic paralysis of the superficial blood vessels. But sugar is not a perfect food. Taken alone it will not support life indefinitely. If taken to the exclusion of a proper amount of nitrogenous food, the subject soon becomes debilitated, and may suffer from fatty degeneration of some important organ. Thus the beer drinker, while he is generally ruddy and in good flesh, may be far from the normal standard of health. With continued excessive drinking of malt liquor, the great accumulation of flesh and purple face show even to the unpracticed eye evidence of serious disease. I cannot do better than to quote from Dr. Norman Kerr the characteristic appearance of the malt liquor drunkard: "In beer and other malt liquor drunkards the subject at an early stage has a tendency to obesity which, as the disease advances, becomes more prominent, till he acquires a bloated appearance, puffing and blowing with the slightest exertion. The features are heavy and dull, the face red and somewhat of a purple hue, with vascular hypertrophy most conspicuous in the region of the eye and nose, with blotches and an oily glistening surface, conjunctival yellowness (bilious or fatty), moist red eyes. In the early stages the beer drinker may be quick and active, but gradually his gait loses much of its elasticity, he looks sluggish and embarrassed in his movements. Dropsy or syncope or embolism frequently closes the scene in middle life."

A peculiar demonstration of the fattening power of sugar in a drunkard was recently brought to my notice by a professional friend. He had under his care for some time an inebriate who drank from forty to sixty glasses of whiskey daily, and, not liking the taste of whiskey, he always poured into the glass an equal amount of plain syrup. This practice he had continued for several years, and when he applied for treatment the flesh hung from nearly all parts of his body in "flabby, yellowish folds," and he was enormously fat.

Again, the beer drinkers of Germany are almost without exception fleshy, while here in America I have seen many beer drinkers decidedly lean; on examination of samples of imported and domestic beers it is found that the German beers do contain more sugar than the domestic article. In some instances, at least, the difference is as great as three or four to one.

The carbon dioxide and bitter principles of the hop give to beer much of its pleasant taste, and probably have some influence in the way of increasing the flow of gastric juice. Tannic acid, on the other hand, of which some beers contain a considerable quantity, has a deleterious influence on digestion. It is a well-known fact that this substance has the property of combining with albumen and the various peptones, forming with them insoluble compounds and thereby perventing their proper digestion and assimilation. Dr. Lambert Ott of Philadelphia, speaking of the acute digestive troubles of beer drinkers, says (Medical News, Jan. 6, 1894) "of one hundred cases of this disease (inflammation of the lining membrane of the stomach) seventy-eight occurred in June, July, and August from pouring cold beer into an empty stomach. In fact, the drinking of beer produces the same disturbances that are produced by any liquor containing alcohol in the same proportion, with the added trouble that comes of tannic acid and the usual adulterations that are in beer." In the beers examined by me the amount of tannic acid varied considerably. Certainly there was enough in some of the specimens examined to produce serious disturbance of the digestive processes.

Of all the alcoholic beverages none are held by the majority of civilized people to have the transcendant virtues of wine. No other food or beverage has commanded so much adulation from all kinds and conditions of men. It occupies so important a place in all the best literatures of the world, in which its desirability, its wholesomeness, its divinity, are the subject of effusive encomium, that to compile a catalogue of its votaries' praises would require a much longer time than is vouchsafed to a single human life. Its worship is sincere and deep rooted, and its worshippers are among the world's greatest and best men. It is amazing, when one stops to consider the matter, how little foundation there is for the average man's opinion as to the value of wine. Good wine, in his estimation, is always desirable. He may abhor drunkenness, look upon the drinking of spirits as dangerous and demoralizing, regard the drinking of malt liquors with contempt; and yet he may consider the drinking of a bottle or more of wine each day as a duty which he owes to his health, his material success in life, or his social position; and he is apt to regard the contents of his wine cellar as one of his greatest treasures. If he is asked the reason for the value he puts upon his wine, he certainly cannot call attention to its intrinsic worth, for he is not a chemist nor a physiologist. His answer must be that it cost him a large price per bottle, that it was made at a famous "Chateau" and that the wines from this place are always high priced; that it was part of the contents of a famous wine cellar which was recently sold, or that it is many years old and came to him through the will of his father, grandfather, or some other relative.

No error, by the way, is more common than that which gives increasing value to wine with increasing age. This value is looked upon as something very real and potent. New wine may be thought unfit to drink. The same wine after ten years is considered good and commands a high price; but let this same wine acquire an age of a hundred years or more, and it now commands a fabulous price and is looked upon as a veritable elixir vitae. One is gravely told even by intelligent men that, no matter in what quantity drunk, such wine is never harmful. It will surely produce drunkenness when taken in sufficient quantity, but even drunkenness produced by it leaves no bad after effects. Good wine is supposed to be tonic and stimulating. Red wine is believed to have the power of making "red blood." Good wine is supposed to be always beneficial. When injury is done by wine it is not the wine which is believed to have done the injury, but the suspicion of adulteration is at once aroused. All the value which the wine possesses may be estimated by considering the substances which enter into its composition. They are water, sugar, tartaric and acetic and a small amount of malic, tannic, and carbonic acids, various salts derived from the grape, like the tartrates of lime and potash, and sulphate of potash and lime, chloride of sodium, potash, and lime. These salts vary in amount from .2 per cent. to .4 per cent. Wine also possesses a peculiar aroma which is known as "bouquet."

The amount of alcohol contained in wines varies from three to thirty or more parts by weight. It is thus seen that some wines may do nearly as much damage as whiskey or brandy. Sugar varies from practically none in the dry wines to twenty-five per cent. or more in the sweetest wines. As sugar is the only constituent of wine possessing a food value, the value of wine as a food will depend upon the amount of sugar it contains. It is quite probable that the malic and acetic acid, and perhaps the tartaric, of wine may aid digestion by reinforcing the gastric juice in cases of insufficiency, and therefore promote gastric digestion.

The bouquet and flavor of wines are due to the development of certain volatile substances by the reaction of acids upon alcohol. These volatile substances belong to the chemical group known as Ethers. In quantity they are intoxicating, and much more injurious than alcohol, but they exist in such small amounts in wine that they serve merely to give its peculiar odor and taste. The development of the bouquet to its fullest extent requires a long time, and this alone makes old wine so much preferred by wine drinkers. In all other respects there is absolutely no difference between old wine and new.

Comparing wine with malt liquor, it will be seen that the latter has more nutritive value than the former because it contains the greater amount of sugar. The sweetest wines, it is true, contain more sugar than the average malt beverage, but sweet wines find little favor with wine drinkers, dry and sour wines being preferred. Champagne contains quite a large percentage of sugar, but its cost limits its use to comparatively few. The wine drunkard is not, therefore, liable to present the bloated, puffy, flabby appearance of the malt liquor drunkard. Wine is also lacking in the bitter principle which gives beer a slight tonic value. Wine has no tonic effect beyond that from the food value of its sugar and the slight aid its acids may give to digestion, and it "stimulates" or narcotizes according to the amount of alcohol it contains.

There is a wide-spread belief that all the common alcoholic beverages are more or less adulterated with harmful substances, and that the damage done by them is not so much due to the beverages themselves as to the poisonous drugs used as adulterants. Many persons willingly drink the currant, grape, and other wines made within the precincts of the household who could not be induced to drink the ordinary article of commerce. Indeed, one frequently hears the praises of the domestic article sounded for its wholesomeness and its purity. A few years ago, when one of the Southern States assumed the duties of dispensing liquors to the public, a great deal of opposition to the plan was silenced by the assurances on the part of the Governor and his followers that under state authority the liquor sold would be pure. Also, in other states in which stringent laws were passed to regulate the liquor traffic, provisions were incorporated to prevent the sale of adulterated liquors, with the hope of lessening the evils attending their consumption. Those who speak of the prevalence of liquor adulterations, however, rarely make any specific charges as to the material used for adulteration purposes. Now and then one hears of spirits being mixed with "impure alcohol," fusel oil, and the like. As a matter of fact, however, the ordinary sophistications of spirits are harmless. They are added with the desire of increasing the bulk, and consequently the profits of the sale of the liquor. For this purpose the most common adulterants are water, to increase the bulk, and caramel or burnt sugar to maintain the proper color; and these not only are not harmful, but render spirituous liquors less irritating by decreasing the amount of alcohol.

While "impure alcohols" are widely spoken of by both physicians and laymen as being used to adulterate liquors, and especially wine, no one has yet pointed out the nature of the impurities. The most common and almost only impurity met with in ethyl alcohol, the ordinary alcohol of commerce, is water. During the process of fermentation, however, other alcohols popularly known as fusel oil are also produced. These have a higher specific gravity and a higher boiling point than ethyl alcohol, but some of them generally pass over with the ethyl alcohol during the process of distillation. With the process of time they are supposed to be oxidized into volatile ethers and so removed. New whiskey, therefore, is supposed to be very injurious because of its contained fusel oil, which is regarded as an especially potent poison. As a matter of fact, recent investigations have shown that there is no warrant for concluding that these heavier alcohols are removed by the process of "aging" of spirituous liquors, and while they are shown to be more irritating than ethyl alcohol, they are by no means as poisonous as they are popularly supposed to be. Recently an English chemist, A. H. Allen, in experiments made on himself, has shown that much larger quantities of fusel oil than any whiskey could contain are borne without any apparent deleterious effect, and a friend of the chemist took a large dose of it without serious after effects.

Many wines are undoubtedly "fortified" by the addition of alcohol, but the alcohol thus used is probably not impure in the sense of being made more harmful. Popularly, also, wines are believed to be colored with haematoxylin and their roughness increased by the addition of alum. No authentic evidence, however, has yet been produced to show that this custom is at all common.

As to the adulteration of beers, a great deal has been

said, and probably with some foundation. Glucose is said to be added to save the expense of using malt, but even if this is true it proves nothing to the detriment of beer, for glucose has the same food value as malt sugar and its products of fermentation are the same. The writer has it on good authority that large amounts of the leaves of some plant or plants are used for the purpose of coloring beer, and some of the beers certainly contain more tannic acid than could be given to them by the usual amount of hops used in brewing. The conclusion arrived at is that the surplus of tannic acid comes from the material used for coloring. Various substances are also said to be used to check fermentation, among them salicylic acid, boracic acid, and formaldehyde. If these latter drugs are used their use is not general, or they are used in very small quantities. The writer did not find them in the beer examined. Tannic acid, however, as has already been pointed out, may exist in quantity sufficient to cause serious digestive disturbances.

A recent French writer, Mr. Joffroy, attaches a good deal of importance to the effects of the by-products of alcoholic fermentation, and declares that they play an important part in determining the pathology of chronic alcoholism (Revue Scientifique, Jan. 15, 1898). He calls attention to the fact that many commercial beverages also contain additions to the ordinary products of fermentation, as absinthe, anisette, vermuth, bitters, and the like; that brandy contains other alcohols than ethyl, aldehydes, and acetic ether. He also calls attention to the various volatile substances and salts found in wine and malt liquor, and argues that those as well as the alcohol must play an important part in producing diseased conditions. There cannot be any doubt that absinthe produces conditions peculiar to itself, and it is likely that aromatics like anise are added to various made beverages in quantity sufficiently large to produce notable effects; but he has produced no evidence to show that the ordinary spirits and wine of commerce contain any of the natural by-products of fermentation in quantity sufficient to cause definite pathological conditions.

In conclusion it must be said that the popular belief in harmful adulterants of common alcoholic beverages is not warranted by any evidence which has thus far been brought to light, and that alcohol alone must be responsible for the damage done by them.

We often hear the remark made that man in his natural state needs alcohol, that there is something lacking in his makeup which alcohol supplies, that he needs a stimulant and that alcohol is the universal natural stimulant. To support this argument the fact that nearly all primitive peoples make beverages containing more or less alcohol is pointed out, and that they readily become fascinated with the effects of the white man's alcoholic beverages when accessible. It would be interesting to know the origin of the alcoholic drinks of each savage people. That they were the result of accident in the first instance can readily be conceived. Savage peoples are noted for their fondness for sugar and sweets of all kinds. What wonder that they should, in their search for vegetable foods, undertake to save up the sweetest juices of various plants for future use, and what wonder that alcoholic fermentation should result therefrom, especially in a tropical or semi-tropical climate? Drinking the juice thus alcoholized, the savage then as to-day found it pleasing in its effects; and he would have to be very low in the scale of intelligence if he would not take the hint and purposely bring about the result which the accident suggested. So here, as it always has been, the appetite did not compel the discovery or invention of the alcoholic beverage; but the beverage created the appetite

It is interesting in this connection to note that neither the Fuegians nor the Eskimos had any alcoholic beverages when discovered by the whites, and do not have any now excepting what they get from traders. There are no plants indigenous to their countries which yield juices rich in sugar, like those of the sugar-cane and the palm. Neither is there any evidence that the great tribes of the central and northern parts of North America understood the art of making alcoholic beverages, of which they are so fond. They had the sap of the sugar maple from which they made sugar, also the sap of the birch and the sugar pine. As the sap from all of them can be gotten only in the early spring, when the snow is still deep on the ground, it is quite likely that the lack of sufficiet warmth to produce fermentation prevented the North American Indian from discovering the secret of alcoholic fermentation.

But primitive peoples have exhibited a "natural" appetite not only for alcohol but for many other forms of narcotic—tobacco, hasheesh, opium, coca erythoxilin, kola, and a variety of other vegetable substances having the power to produce pleasing intoxication. There can be scarcely any doubt that the narcotic taking of savages when it is not attended by religious rites is induced by that desire for blissful oblivion of the hard conditions of life which makes the civilized brother drown his sorrows in the wine-cup.

XVIII.

Shall the Physician Cease to Prescribe Alcohol.

There is no doubt that alcohol as a remedial agent might be forever banished from the physician's armamentarium of drugs without in any way lessening his efficiency in combating disease. Indeed, his hands would be strengthened thereby, for now he relies upon the fictitious food and stimulant value of alcohol to the exclusion of safer and infinitely better remedies. This is not mere theory. It is confirmed by no less an authority than Benjamin Ward Richardson, one of the acutest observers and most philosophic and original physicians of the century.

In 1892, fifteen years after he had virtually retired from hospital practice, he was invited to become physician to the London Temperance Hospital, where he was left free to prescribe alcohol medicinally in all cases and at all times that he might see fit. This gave him the opportunity which he had long wished for to treat various diseases without alcohol in any quantity or form. In his own words, he declares this invitation "was so much to my taste, and the mode in which it came so handsomely conceived, that I could not help availing myself of it." Here he treated two hundred successive cases of serious diseases extending over a wide range in variety and affecting persons of different social conditions, without using a drop of alcohol in a single case. Instead of the ordinary alcoholic tinctures he used glycerine and certain prepared waters as menstrua for the solution of active drugs. These waters were aqua opii, aqua ferri, aqua chloroformi, and others. His results were all that could be desired. Certainly they could not have been made better by the use of alcohol in any way.

But many other physicians before and since the experience of Dr. Richardson have treated diseases of all kinds without the use of alcohol, and their reports surely do not indicate that any thing was lost by leaving it out of the list of drugs exhibited.

The narcotic effects of alcohol should make it of value in selected cases. A small quantity of it well diluted, at bedtime, has a decided and pleasing hypnotic effect with certain nervous individuals troubled by insomnia, but the liability of contracting a habit under such circumstances is very great—so great that the thoughtful physician would be very sure of his patient before subjecting him to the seductive influences of so pleasing a remedy. If the sale of alcohol were surrounded by the same safeguards that surround the sale of other powerful narcotic poisons, the danger would be much lessened, but it is the most easily procurable of all merchandise. Some form of hypnotic less palatable and less easily procured should take the place of alcohol. The method of prescribing alcohol, too, is open to serious objections. Instead of receiving a prescription instructing a druggist to furnish a solution containing a definite percentage of alcohol and directing that a definite dose be taken at stated times, the patient is instructed to buy a case of wine, beer, or spirits, as the case may be, and use it as a beverage. Certainly this method is responsible for the making of many drunkards.

As a remedy for the relief of pain alcohol is so inferior to many other standard drugs that its use for this purpose need not be considered. No objection should be offered to the use of alcohol as a solvent for powerful drugs. For this purpose no other substance is so well adapted, for not only are nearly all vegetable substances freely soluble in this menstruum, but it serves the important purpose of preventing drug deterioration by fermentation, and the small amount of alcohol used in making tinctures, or added for the purpose of preservation, need excite no apprehension.

XIX.

The Effects of Alcohol on Civilization.

When a physiological chemist wishes to ascertain the probable amount of damage done by any poison which has been introduced into the circulation of an animal, he must first know the potency of the poison and the amount of tissue to be affected. To make the matter more explicit, he must know, for instance, how many grains of the drug are necessary per kilogram of animal weight to produce a fatal issue. He must know, moreover, how much damage is done and to what organs by a quantity not large enough to kill. This he learns by experimentation, by producing various degrees of toxicity extending over various periods of time, finally killing the animal experimented upon and subjecting its tissues to a searching examination. The toxic action of alcohol on the human tissues is unfortunately already too well known, but in order to arrive at a probable estimate of the total damage done to the population as a whole, we must know how much of the poison is consumed, and by how many individuals.

One of the most persistently reiterated statements in medical literature is that two fluid ounces of alcohol may be "burned up" in the body if taken at intervals, in small doses, during a day of twenty-four hours. This would equal one grain of absolute alcohol to one kilogram of weight in a man of one hundred and fifty pounds weight, an amount which Dujuardin-Baumetz found could be given to pigs "without being followed by any pathologic changes." Anstie put the amount one-sixth less. As a matter of fact, however, there is no reason for thinking that two ounces of alcohol ingested daily might not produce serious disturbances in susceptible individuals, but, as it seems to be accepted by the medical profession as a truth, it may be used as a basis of estimation in this place.

For the total amount of alcohol consumed in any year we may consult the industrial statistics of the United States government. Here it is found that the total consumption of alcoholic beverages, domestic and imported, were for the year 1896 as follows:

Spirits	71,051,967 gallons
Wines	18,701,406 gallons
Malt Liquors	1,080,626,164 gallons

Estimating the spirits to contain 53% of alcohol, the wine an average of 15%, and the malt liquors an average of 4%, we get the following amounts of alcohol consumed in that year as follows:

In the spirits	37,657,542 gallons
In the wine	2,805,211 gallons
In the malt liquors	48,628,177 gallons
Total	89,090,930 gallons

Taking the population of the country in 1896 in round numbers at seventy millions, the per capita consumption of absolute alcohol for that year would equal 1.27 gallons.

But what percentage of the total population must be charged with drinking this enormous quantity of alcohol? That question is not easily answered. Here in America women and children rarely drink alcoholic beverages.

They may therefore be eliminated as consumers of alcohol. Of the adult males, taking the urban and rural population together, one-half, probably, drink more or less of some kind of alcoholic drink. Estimating the adult males as one-fifth of the total population, or twenty per cent, this would give ten per cent of the total population as alcohol consumers. A medical man with whom this subject was discussed, thought this estimate too low— in his opinion, fifteen to twenty per cent of the total populaion would be nearer the truth. Certainly, however, the number of all occasional and constant drinkers of alcoholic liquors cannot be greater than twenty per cent, or one out of every five, of the total population.

If ten per cent of the total population drink all the alcohol consumed in the ordinary beverages, this would give to each individual 12.7 gallons per annum, or 1625.6 ounces, a daily quantity of 4.45 ounces or more than twice as much as the maximum quantity which is said to be eliminated from the human body without damage.

Taking the large percentage as representing the alcohol consumers, one out of every five of the total population, the daily amount of alcohol, 2.224 ounces, would still exceed the safe maximum. This method of reasoning, however, does little more than hint at the destructive possibilities of alcohol. As a matter of fact, there is nothing even approximating this equal distribution of alcohol among all those who indulge in any degree in alcoholic beverages. It would, probably, be very near the truth to say that three per cent of the population consume at least sixty per cent of the total amount of alcohol consumed, and that two and a quarter millions of our people, mostly adult males, are being rapidly destroyed by its poisonous effects, and that this destruction is going on constantly. To this should be added, probably, at least half as large a number of victims of hereditary alcoholic degeneration.

The latent capabilities of this ninety million gallons of alcohol consumed in the beverages of seventy million people during the year 1896 can be better illustrated by showing how many adult lives could be destroyed by that amount of the poison.*

Considering one pint of the absolute alcohol the average lethal dose (it is probably much less than that), there would be enough in the ninety million gallons to furnish ten and a half fatal doses to each individual within the borders of our country. But one pint is a lethal dose for an adult. A much less quantity would suffice to destroy the life of a child. There was, therefore, enough alcohol drank every two or three weeks during that year to destroy the entire population if it had been taken within an hour. There is a general belief that the consumption of alcohol is decreasing. This belief is based upon the fact that the per capita consumption of spirits shows a slight decrease when compared with that of ten and twenty years ago. As a matter of fact, however, the rapid increase in the quantity of malt liquors consumed makes a steady increase in the total alcoholic consumption. The following table shows the nature and extent of that increase by comparing the consumption of 1886 and 1876. As the change in the per capita consumption of wine during these years was very slight, it will not be considered. In the three years mentioned there was the following per capita consumption of alcohol:

---

*The lethal dose of alcohol seems to have received but little attention from medical men. Kayser, quoted by Demme (Einfluss des Alkohols auf den Organismus des Kindes, P. 13), reported the death of a three-year-old child following the Ingestion of 75 grams (2.3 ounces) of undiluted alcohol. A fatal issue followed the drinking of 330 grams (10.3 ounces) by an adult.

Demme believes that smaller doses than these would probably cause death at these periods of life.

1876—Spirits..... 1.33 gallons, 92.88 ounces alcohol
    Malt liquors. 6.83 gallons, 34.97 ounces alcohol
    Total...... 8.16 gallons, 127.85 ounces alcohol
1886—Spirits...... 1.26 gallons, 85.45 ounces alcohol
    Malt liquors. 11.20 gallons, 57.34 ounces alcohol
    Total...... 12.46 gallons, 142.79 ounces alcohol
1896—Spirits...... 1.00 gallons, 67.84 ounces alcohol
    Malt liquors. 15.16 gallons, 77.62 ounces alcohol
    Total...... 16.16 gallons, 145.46 ounces alcohol

Comparing the per capita consumption of 1876 and 1886, there is an increase of a little more than 11.5 per cent in the total alcohol consumption, while a comparison of 1886 with 1896 gives an increase of something less than 2 per cent. It will thus be seen that the per capita consumption of absolute alcohol has increased about 14 per cent in twenty years. Taking the average yearly per capita consumption of the two decades, the showing is much less favorable. The former shows an average per capita consumption of spirits amounting to 1.306 gallons and the latter 1.336 gallons, an increase instead of a decrease, of .03 gallon. The increase in the average per capita consumption of malt liquors during the same time was enormous. During the decade 1876-85 it was only 8.57 gallons, while in the decade 1886-95 it was 13.82. Thus the per capita consumption of absolute alcohol averaged about 70 per cent more for the years of the second decade than for the years of the first decade. During this same time the per capita consumption of wine averaged, for the first decade, .465 gallon, and for the second, .459 gallon annually, a decrease of only .006 gallon in the second decade. From these figures it will be seen that, while we still continue to drink our spirits and wine in practically the same amount that we did twenty years ago, we have enormously increased our annual supply of malt liquors, so those who think that the rapid increase in beer consumption is lessening the drink evil are laboring under a delusion.

No doubt this enormous increase in the consumption of malt liquor is due to the old and carefully fostered error that beer is a harmless beverage, and that if beer could be substituted for potable liquids containing a larger percentage of alcohol, the cause of temperance would be practically won. It is difficult to say how old this fraud may be. Away back in the colonial days of New England the brewing industry was fostered and encouraged by a law exempting from taxes and giving a prize to any brewer who should produce more than five hundred barrels of beer annually. In some parts of New England the sale of light alcoholic drinks is still favored by the law, requiring a much smaller license fee from saloons in which beer, wine, and cider only are sold. In Boston prior to 1886 a license of $250 was required from sellers of these beverages, "it having been urged that it was in the interest of temperance to encourage the use of malt liquors and thereby decrease the consumption of distilled spirits" (The Liquor Problem, by the Committee of Fifty, P. 198). So we find on every hand not only laymen but physicians urging the encouraging of beer drinking as a temperance measure. A recent article by a medical man (Journal of the Am. Med. Assn., Feb. 19, 1898) contains the following statement: "In the writer's judgment it would be wise for the government to put upon the manufacture of spirits used as a beverage the highest excise duties compatible with collection, a moderate excise on fermented liquors derived from grain and hops, and to encourage the production of light table wines by leaving them free."

For the refutation of this error, as in the case of all

popular errors on medical subjects, we need only go to those men whose opinions are based upon exact methods of investigation. Kerr, quoting Dujardin-Baumetz and Audigé, says (Alcoholism and Drug Habits) "the more concentrated the alcoholic liquor ingested the more intense the inflammation of tissue. *At the same time an equal quantity of the potable alcohols will sooner exhibit their characteristic symptoms if largely diluted with water.* All alcohols are poisons. All alcoholic influence is the same in kind, varying only in degree. The common belief that there is no wine or beer, but only spirituous, inebriety is an error. Of the inebriates treated at the Dalrymple Home in England, eight per cent have been wine or beer drinkers."

Says one of Germany's most eminent physicians in a recently published pamphlet (Dr. Adolph von Struempell, Ueber die Alkoholfrage vom aertztlichen Standpunkt aus, 1898) "when we see year after year a not insignificant number of respected men, skillful in their calling, sicken and die when sickness and death certainly are chiefly or exclusively due to the supposedly innocent habit of drinking from two to three liters of beer daily, should it not be the earnest care of the physician to call attention to this dangerous habit?" Says the same author again (Loc. Cit., P. 15) "Nothing is from the physician's standpoint more false than to think that the evil influence of alcohol is lessened through the increased substitution of beer for the stronger alcoholic drinks." It is under the deceptive mask of a pleasant tasting and nutritious beverage, as beer, that alcohol finds its way into circles otherwise completely closed to it.

Certainly another important fact cannot be too often reiterated. That is, that an overwhelming majority of all inebriates or drunkards begin their downward career with beer and wine tippling. As a rule, the stronger alcoholic liquors are regularly indulged in only after a necessity or desire for alcoholic narcotism has been produced by the drinking of beverages containing smaller percentages of alcohol. When this stage in the tippler's career is reached, he no longer seeks to quench his thirst with a beverage, but to supply the demands of a depraved nervous system with its accustomed poison.

Let no one, then, be cajoled into believing that the drinking of beer should be encouraged as a temperance measure; for not only has the enormous increase in the per capita consumption of beer not lessened that of spirituous liquors, but, even should the former totally displace the latter, nothing would be gained unless the total per capita consumption of alcohol should be decreased. In short, we shall gain nothing for the welfare and advancement of civilization by substituting beer drunkards for whiskey drunkards.

From an economic point of view the drink habit is ruinously expensive. Taking again the amount of alcoholic beverages consumed in the year 1896 we find the following probable amount paid by the consumer:

Spirits—71,051,967 gallons at .50 per pint.. $284,207,868
Wines—18,701,406 gallons at .50 per quart.   37,402,812
Malt liquors—1,080,626,164 gal. .10 per pint 944,500,931

Total $1,266,111,611

This estimate is probably too low. Sold over the bar of the saloonkeeper, the average drink of spirits is perhaps not more than one and a half ounces, which sells at an average price of ten cents. This would make a pint sell for something more than a dollar, making no allowance for the almost universal adulteration with water after it reaches the hands of the saloonkeeper. Much beer and wine, as well as spirits, is bought in bulk by the customer at figures lower than those given here, but there is to offset this the higher price paid in the public houses where the greater part of these beverages is consumed. Taken altogether, the total amount spent by the customers cannot be less than that here indicated; 1,266 millions of dollars is an enormous sum of money. It is about equal to one-half of the nation's greatest public debt. It is one and a quarter times the indemnity paid to Germany by France at the close of the Franco-Prussian war. It is more than one-half the total money now in circulation in the United States. So great is the amount of wealth represented by these figures that it would have sufficed to pay more than one-half the wages of all the factory employes of the United States in the year 1890. And what does the consumer get for this sum of money? A very small amount of food material mixed with a relatively large amount of poison. The food material, if it were separated from the other ingredients, would be dear at one-twentieth of that which was paid for the beverages, but, as a matter of fact, its value, small as it was, was entirely destroyed by the admixture of the poison. *We are now engaged in a costly war with Spain. Our expenses may amount to anywhere from six hundred to a thousand million dollars before it is ended. Economical citizens mention this great sum and groan at the prospective burden of taxation. But by this war we shall gain honor, respect, and a magnificent national solidarity, which will make those millions a profitable investment, and the burden of investment will rest lightly upon the shoulders of a prosperous and happy people. Let us

*This was written in the summer of 1898. As a matter of fact our expenses in the war with Spain were only about one-fifth of the amount paid for alcohol beverages in 1896, and we have gained all the advantages mentioned here, and more.

rather turn our attention to twice that great number of millions, which is a self-imposed burden upon the shoulders of a few millions of people and brings no return but poverty, misery, sickness, and death.

Of peculiar interest is the fact that three-fourths of the total amount spent for alcoholic beverages went for malt liquor, nearly all of which was domestic beer. This means, of course, that the workingman paid the largest part of this enormous saloon bill, for he is by far the most important consumer of beer. For this purpose he spends a considerable part of his income. Here in America, among the workingmen of cities at least, it cannot be less than ten per cent. Perhaps fifteen or sixteen per cent would be nearer the truth. Of the amount thus spent in Germany, Von Struempell says (Die Alkoholfrage, P. 5) "I have through thorough inquiry very often convinced myself that the laborer who receives three marks daily for his services spends fifty pfennigs for beer for his own use, that is, about one-sixth of his entire income." With us wages are higher and the necessities of life cheaper, consequently there is an incentive to spend more for beer. Certainly an amount is thus spent sufficient, if it were invested in dividend paying life insurance or some other form of accumulating investment, to guard against all the ordinary exigencies of misfortune and prevent the workingman and his children from ever becoming public charges.

But human lives and money are not the only forms of wealth which are sacrificed to alcohol. The amount of human effort which is dissipated in the production, distribution, and consumption of alcoholic beverages is simply incalculable, and it is as absolutely thrown away as though the individuals who manufacture and distribute them and those who spend their time in drinking them

THE EFFECTS OF ALCOHOL ON CIVILIZATION. 187

and waiting for the paralyzing effects of alcohol to be dissipated were members of a standing army quartered upon the people. Alcoholic beverages possess no economic value aside from the small amount of food material found in malt liquors and wines. It should be remembered, however, that the grain and fruit used in the production of these has many times the value of the manufactured articles, while that used in making distilled liquors is a total loss as food for human beings.

The size of this army, which were better idle, is not easily estimated. The census of 1890 gives 50,000 as the number engaged in brewing alone. Probably there are at least as many more engaged in the manufacture of distilled spirits and wine. How many are directly engaged in the liquor traffic? As no statistics are at hand, the number can only be estimated. If there is one saloon for every five hundred inhabitants (and this estimate is not too high) we have about 140,000 saloons, the care of which occupies the whole time of at least 200,000 men. But beside the saloonkeeper there are others engaged in the liquor traffic, wholesalers, traveling salesmen, and the like, to the extent of at least 30,000 men. By far the greatest loss of time, however, is that suffered by the consumer, and it is more difficult to estimate. An interesting attempt in this direction was made by the Committee of Fifty last year in Boston. Here 606 saloons received in the aggregate 226,752 visits daily. Suppose that each visit consumed ten minutes of time. Then there was spent in the saloons of Boston 37,792 hours each day, equal to the idleness of 3,779 men, allowing ten hours for a working day. Boston has a population of about a half million. At the same rate of time expenditure, the whole United States has an army of over 500,000, nearly all adult males, spending all their time in drinking alcoholic beverages.

It may be objected that much of this time is given outside of working hours. This is true, but it should also be remembered that the mere time spent in drinking is not the only factor of loss, perhaps not even the most important one. There still remains to be considered the time actually lost by incapacity for labor, brought about not only by acute alcoholic poisoning, but also by the scores of physical ailments thus engendered, which lessen or completely destroy the productive capabilities of the drinkers, and these would, without doubt, much more than offset the time spent outside of working hours.

To sum up, then, the army devoted to the interests of alcoholic beverages is made up as follows:

Manufacturers.............................. 100,000
Wholesalers and traveling salesmen............. 30,000
Retailers.................................. 200,000
Drinkers.................................. 500,000

Total............................ 830,000

This estimate, then, gives us an army approximating a million men who contribute nothing of economic value to the nation and who are supported by the productive industries, a number equal to about six per cent of the adult male population.

But the expense does not stop here. There is still to be considered the enormously costly machinery of legal procedure made necessary by the increase in crime which is directly traceable to brain deterioration resulting from alcoholic intoxication, asylums for dependent children, pauper institutions, insane asylums, and prisons, all of which are so largely recruited from the ranks of drunkards and their descendants, making altogether an expense which must consume the product of many hundred thousand individuals. Would it be too much to say that at least ten per cent of our industrial efforts are completely neutralized by the pernicious habit of alcohol drinking?

The increase in alcohol consumption in European countries is a matter of grave importance. In Germany for the years 1872 to 1875 there was an average per capita consumption of 67.3 liters of beer and 8.6 liters of spirits. This amount increased in the next five years until in 1881 the consumption of beer was 87.6 and of spirits 9.2 liters per capita. In Prussia alone in 1872, 57.4 liters of beer and 12. liters of spirits was the per capita consumption. In 1875 the amount had risen to 60.3 liters of beer and 14.9 liters of spirits per capita. The increase in the number of saloons has kept even pace with the increase in consumption (August Smith, Die Alkoholfrage, P. 107). The per capita consumption of alcoholic beverages for all the German Empire in 1896 was according to Bade as follows: Beer 108.5 liters, spirits 13.2, and wine 6.44 liters. A liter is 2.113 pints. Estimating a liter at one quart, the per capita consumption in gallons would be, approximately, beer 27.1 gallons, spirits 3.3 gallons, and wine 1.61 gallons, more than twice as great as the per capita consumption in America, estimated as absolute alcohol.

The amount of illness and death for which alcohol is responsible is well set forth in statistics gathered by Dr. Smith. In Switzerland, during the last few years, the name and cause of the disease producing death in every case is given on a death card filled out by the attending physician, without giving the name of the patient. From these, tolerably correct reports of the percentage of deaths from alcohol have been obtained. The result of these statistics for the years 1891 and 1892, for the fifteen largest cities of Switzerland give the following: Of all males of 20 years of age or over dying in 1891, 10.7 per cent and in 1892, 10.8 per cent, died of alcohol poisoning. In the same years the percentage of females dying from the same cause was 1.7 and 2 per cent, respectively.

Because of the similar ways of living, and especially of the rapid increase in spirits consumption in the provinces of Posen and Schlesien, the result in Germany, thinks Smith, is at least as bad as that in Switzerland, and probably the death rate is higher. That is, every ninth individual in Germany dies of alcoholic poisoning.

If it be objected that these statistics are insufficient and that the number of deaths from alcoholism in these two years was accidental and not to be considered the average for any considerable time, attention is called for further proof to the mortality statistics, against which these objections cannot be urged, of certain life insurance companies. In some English insurance companies the total abstainers are put in a separate class and receive more favorable rates than the moderate drinkers. Here it has been found that the death rate of the total abstainers is about 30 per cent less than that of those who are classed as occasional or moderate drinkers. Taking the statistics of the "United Kingdom Temperance and General Provident Institution" in the years 1886 to 1891:

	Unclassified	Abstinence Class
Estimated deaths	7,763	5,177
Actual deaths	7,459	3,663

That is, the actual number of deaths in the occasional drinkers was 97.33% of the expectation, while the actual number in the abstinence class was only 70.75% of the expectation.

Still more convincing is the showing of the statistics for 1884 to 1889 of the "Scepter," the clients of which are mostly ministers of the gospel and members of various religious orders, which is as follows:

	Unclassified	Abstinence Class
Expected deaths	569	240
Actual deaths	434	143

Here the actual deaths of the first class were 76.27% of the expectation, and of the second class only 57.42%.

In the year 1893, in the former company, the deaths reached 100, 85% of the expectation, in the unclassified, while among the abstinence class it was only 71.62% of the expectation. In the latter company the results correspond with those of the former. In consequence of the favorable showing in the death rate of the total abstainers these companies give them a discount of 8 or 10% on their premiums, and notwithstanding this discrimination they are better risks than the unclassified.

Returning to the mortality statistics of Switzerland as exhibited by the death cards already referred to, the influence of alcohol is as perceptible as in those of the insurance companies. Taking the mortality of all males over twenty years of age by twenty year periods and comparing the number of deaths from alcohol with the whole number, the following table is the result:

	Total Deaths.			Deaths from Alcohol.		
1891	3499			366		
1892	3343			361		
Ages	20–39	40–59	Over 60	20–39	40–59	Over 60
1891	27 %	36.3%	36.7%	29.2%	50 %	20.6%
1892	25.5%	38.3%	36.3%	22.7%	55.7%	21.6%

Analyzing the above table, it will be seen that while the first group shows practically the same percentage of mortality in deaths from alcohol as is shown in the total number of deaths, in the second group the percentage of mortality in the subjects of alcoholism is enormously increased. This is undoubtedly due to the fact that the first period is given to preparing a way, through degeneration processes, for rapid dissolution after the fortieth year, from tuberculosis and other masked diseases. Thus at the very time of life when the man is of greatest value to his family and to the state he is destroyed by a system of chronic alcoholic suicide.

The influence of moderate drinking in the production of increased morbidity is well illustrated by the statistics collected by Carpenter relating to British soldiers in the Indian service. Observations were made upon 17,354 moderate drinkers and 9,340 abstinent soldiers. Of the former group one out of every 7.28 men was sent to the hospital, but of the latter group only one out of every 14.47. Still more favorable to the abstinence group are the statistics considering the average number of days spent in the hospital. The average number of sick days of every hundred moderate drinkers was 10.20, while the average of the abstainers was 3.64 sick days for every hundred.

The experience of certain benefit associations in England gives very similar results. In three of these (Mutual Experience Rural Towns and City Districts, Mutual Experience Rural Districts, and Foresters), in the five years, 1884 to 1889, for each laborer, there were 26.20, 24.68, and 27.66 weeks of illness, an average of 26.18 weeks while at the same time in the "Sons of Temperance," which receives only total abstainers, the number of weeks of illness for every member was only 7.48, less than one-third of the others.

Here we have a remarkably close agreement between statistics taken from widely separated communities and under very different circumstances, and from them it would appear that two-thirds of the total amount of illness

THE EFFECTS OF ALCOHOL ON CIVILIZATION. 193

is to be ascribed to alcohol alone. Moreover, it is evident, and practical experience long ago established, that alcoholic indulgence is able to make otherwise trifling illness serious, short illness long, and cause a fatal issue in serious cases which might otherwise have recovered.

Another way in which civilization is affected by alcohol is the amount of crime for which it is directly responsible. To adequately discuss the relationship of alcoholism and crime would require much more space than can be given to it in a work of this kind. Nothing more will be done here, therefore, than to indicate the probable percentage of criminal acts for which alcohol is directly responsible. Statistics on this subject should not be taken too implicitly. As information regarding previous habits of the criminal generally come from the crminal himself, they are not always trustworthy. With a view of obtaining a light sentence or an early pardon, the prisoner is liable to hide much of the truth regarding his habits, and put himself in as favorable a light as possible before the public. On the other hand, the criminal often seeks to excuse his conduct by untruthfully asserting that he was drunk at the time the crime was committed.

Some statistics may be produced, however, which fairly show how much crime may be directly attributed to alcohol drinking, both in America and Europe. The most complete statistics yet compiled in America upon this subject are those embraced in the Twenty-sixth Annual Report of the Bureau of Statistics of Labor of Massachusetts, for the year ending August 20, 1895. During this time there were accomplished, within the state, 26,672 convictions, 17,573 of which were for drunkenness alone, and 650 for drunkenness united with other crimes. Eliminating the convictions for drunkeness and for drunkenness with other crimes, there remain 8,449 convictions for other crimes to be investigated. Of this number, from nine only was no information obtained as to whether the convict was under the influence of liquor at the time the crime was committed. Of the remaining 8,440, an affirmative answer was given in 3,640 cases, and in 4,791 cases the convict replied that he was not under the influence of alcohol at the time that the crime was committed. In other words, out of the total number of convictions 68.73% were directly due to drunkenness or to drunkenness with other crimes, and 81.97% of the criminal convictions were for criminal acts committed while the convict was under the influence of alcohol, leaving only 18.03% of all the convictions not directly traceable to alcoholic intoxication.

Examining the convictions for crimes against persons we obtain the following results: For murder and manslaughter there were 21 convictions, and 12 of the offenses, or 57%, were committed while the convict was under the influence of alcohol; 61 cases of assault with a weapon, 31 of which were due to alcohol; 69 cases of assault upon an officer, with 36 due to alcoholic intoxication; 12 cases of felonious assault, 3 of which were committed under the influence of alcohol; and 1,652 cases of assault and battery, of which 985 were influenced by alcoholic intoxication. For robbery there were 46 convictions, 38 of which were committed by men under the influence of liquor. It will thus be seen that about 50% of the cases of serious assault, 67% of the cases of assault and battery, and 82% of the cases of conviction for highway robbery, were for offenses committed while the criminal was under the influence of alcoholic intoxication. Of crimes against property, 1,137 persons out of a total number of 2,107 convicted of larceny, or nearly 54%, were under the influence of alcoholic drink at the time the offense was committed, and of incendiarism and malicious mis-

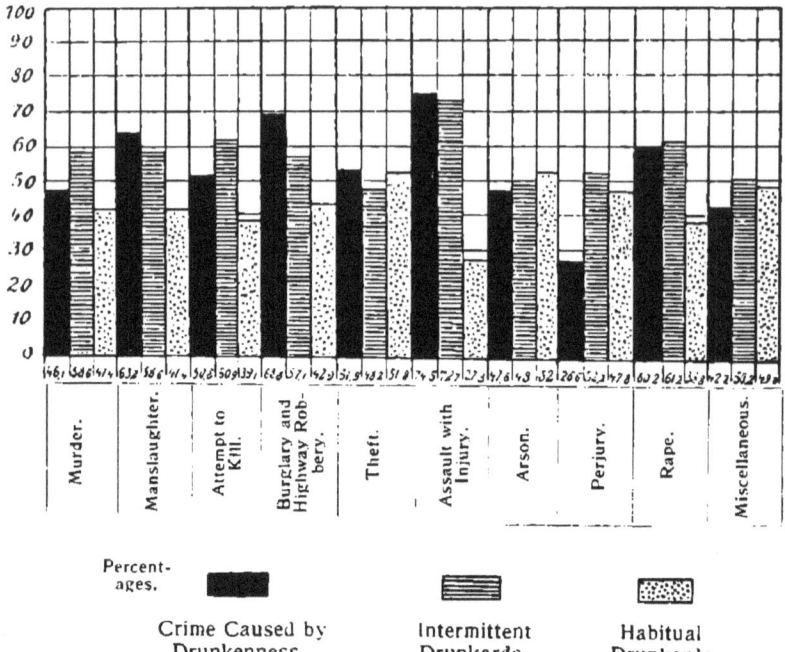

FIG. 4.

RELATION OF DRUNKENNESS TO CRIME.

Penitentiaries for Men.

Crime Caused by Drunkenness.   Intermittent Drunkards.   Habitual Drunkards.

NOTE—The black column represents the *total* percentage of crime caused by drunkenness. The other two columns represent the *relative* amount of alcoholic crime committed by the intermittent and habitual drunkard respectively.

FIG. 5.

Houses of Correction for Men.

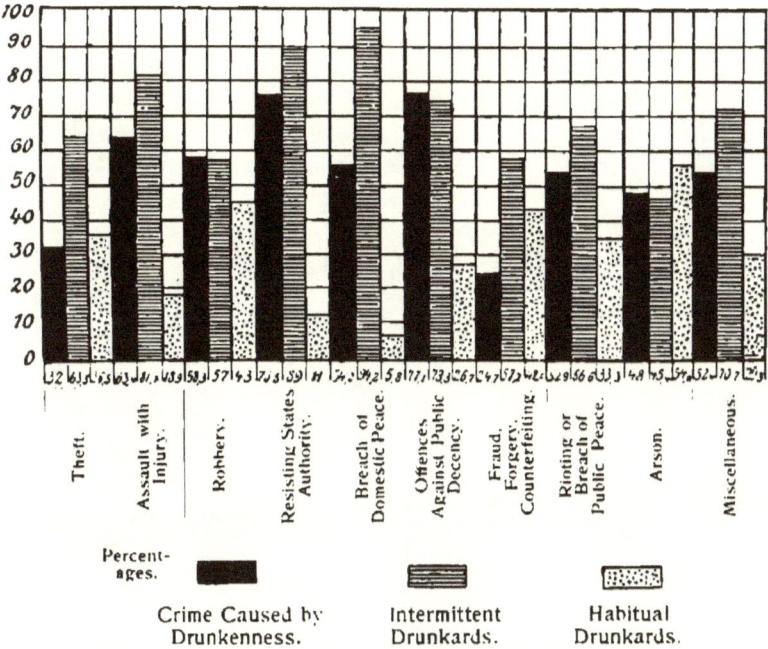

NOTE—The black column represents the *total* percentage of crime caused by drunkenness. The other two columns represent the *relative* amount of alcoholic crime committed by the intermittent and habitual drunkard respectively.

THE EFFECTS OF ALCOHOL ON CIVILIZATION. 195

chief, 33% and 66% respectively were to be attributed to alcoholic intoxication.

On the other hand, crimes against the authority of the state, like fraud, embezzlement, selling liquor without a license, counterfeiting, polygamy—crimes unaccompanied by personal violence—were not committed as a rule by drunkards, the percentages being 7, 28, 14, 0 and 26 respectively.

Very similar were the results obtained by Baer and reported at an international prison congress in 1874. The report covered 120 prisons and houses of correction which contained 32,837 male convicts. Of this number, 13,706 attributed their criminal career directly to the influence of alcohol. Two classes of penal institutions were investigated—jails, houses of correction, and similar prisons, and penitentiaries—and a separate report made for each class. The convicts were classified according to the nature of the crime committed, and, furthermore, divided into occasional and habitual drunkards. The following tables (Figs. 4 and 5) arranged by Dr. August Smith of Baden (Die Alkoholfrage, P. 9) show at a glance the percentage of drunken criminals as compared with the whole number in each class of criminal offenses, and also the relative number of occasional and habitual drunkards among the convicts addicted to alcoholic intoxication. Of the 13,706 convicts given to alcoholic excesses, 7,262 were periodic or occasional drunkards, while 6,437 were habitual drunkards.

It will be seen from Dr. Smith's table that 46.1% of the cases of murder and 63.2% of the cases of manslaughter were influenced by alcoholic intoxication, giving an average of 54.1% for the total homicides, differing only by 3% from the result obtained in Massachusetts. Further comparison between the two groups of statistics shows a like similarity throughout. Take, for instance, assault with intent to kill or do great bodily harm, assault and battery, and robbery and highway robbery. The Massachusetts statistics give 50%, 67%, and 82%, while Dr. Smith's tables give 50.8%, 68.4% (63.4% in table I and 74.5 in table II), and 68.8% respectively, as having been directly caused by alcoholic intoxication. A comparison of all the other crimes in the two groups of statistics show very closely approximating results. It should not be forgotten, however, that the Massachusetts statistics are based upon the question as to whether the convict was under the influence of alcohol at the time the offense was committed, while those collected by Baer are based upon the convict's drinking habits as a whole, without regard to his condition at the particular time the crime was actually committed. This fact is sufficient to account for the differences in percentages of those crimes which are not accompanied by violence. Crimes like embezzlement, fraud, and counterfeiting have been initiated by necessity arising from the wastefulness of drinking habits, but the crimes themselves could scarcely be successfully carried out by one under the influence of alcohol.

An important part is played in criminal statistics by the occasional or periodic drunkard. In all deeds of violence he has won a bad eminence, and his moral degeneration, his insensibility to public decency and morality, is scarcely less marked. It is seen from Baer's statistics that of all the deeds of violence for which alcohol can be held directly responsible the occasional drunkard committed 58.6% of the homicides, 60.9% of the attempts to kill, 72.7% and 81.4% of the assaults with injury, 89% of the cases of resistance to the state's authority, 94.2% of breach of domestic peace, and 73.3% of the offenses against public morals. Indeed, the statistics show just what ought to be expected, and just what is happening

FIG. 6.

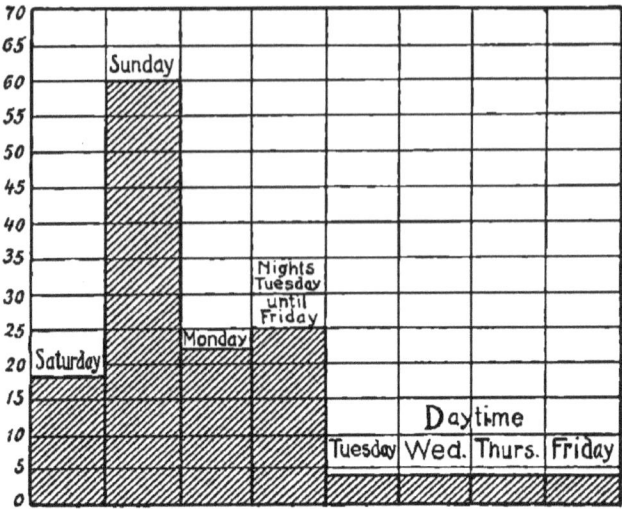

Table showing the relative number of crimes against persons on the different days of the week, and on the nights of Tuesday to Friday inclusive, for which conviction was secured in the court of Judge Lang (adopted from A. Smith's "Die Alkoholfrage").

THE EFFECTS OF ALCOHOL ON CIVILIZATION. 197

in the daily experience of all peoples who drink alcoholic beverages—namely, that a sudden access of alcoholic intoxication produces a species of mania characterized, usually, by homicidal tendencies. Moreover, if statistics were collected concerning the crimes of habitual drunkards, they would certainly show that most of them were also brought about by the same kind of mania due to an imbibition of an increased quantity of alcohol.

An interesting investigation showing the connection of alcoholism and crime was made by Judge Lang of Zurich in 1890. The statistics collected by him showed that acts of violence against persons and property were committed mostly between Saturday evening and Monday evening, and that this increase was coincident with an increase in alcoholic consumption. The following diagram (Fig. 6) shows the relative proportion of cases of assault with bodily injury for the different days of the week, and for Tuesday, Wednesday, Thursday, and Friday nights. Of 141 convictions for this offense, only 41 were committed "on the 208 days of the year on which, according to a ruling custom, less is drunk" than during other times. The other 100 offenses were committed on the 157 days upon which an increased amount of alcohol was consumed, and of the 41 convictions above mentioned, 25 were for offenses committed in or near a saloon at night, while in only 16 cases was there no evidence that alcohol had anything to do with the crime.

Said Lord Coleridge of England: "If the English people could be made temperate nine-tenths of the English prisons could be closed."

Said Dr. Krohne, director of penal institutions in Germany, in a public address delivered a few years ago: "Of crimes against life and limb, assault, assault with bodily injury, manslaughter, and attempts to commit murder nearly the entire number is chargeable to drunkenness. Crimes against property are almost without exception the result of necessity, and in 80% of the cases the necessity which led to the crime is the result of drunkenness. Crimes against morality are almost exclusively caused by alcoholic beverages. This has been my experience in a service of twenty years in Oldenburg, Schleswig-Holstein, Hesse, and Brandenburg. Seventy per cent of all deeds of violence against property rights are, more or less, the result of alcohol drinking. Two years ago I received a visit from a friend who had just served as a juryman in Wuerzburg, and he remarked that it was a significant fact that every crime which had been tried during his service was the result, direct or indirect, of alcoholic intoxication."

Think, too, the extent to which the habit of alcoholic intoxication prevents the highest realization of physical and mental capability and the nation's loss arising therefrom. Said a recent well-known writer on economic subjects (Walter A. Wyckoff in "The Workers"):

"Men . . . . who have risen by force of ambition and sheer development of manual skill to good position in the factory and have there stood still, their congenital qualities incapable, presumably of higher efficiency. But sadder far than theirs is the case of men who are often best endowed with native cleverness and aptitude, who rise quickly in the scale of promotion, and who might rise far higher than they do but for the cause of careless living. They know no interest in their work nor pleasure in its doing. To them it is the sordid drudgery by which they gain the means of gratifying their real purpose and desires. With sullen perseverance they endure the torment of labor, with pay day in view and then Saturday night and Sunday spend all in their mad revels in what they call life."

But over and above all, and far more important than all the material losses chargeable to the universal imbibition of beverages poisoned with alcohol, has been the effect which alcohol has had upon the ethics of civilization, upon the ideals and conduct of man in his intercourse with his fellows. These alcohol has immeasurably lowered. All classes and phases of society have suffered thereby. In the family, where the breadwinner should also give love and protection to the weak members of society and carefully train them in the duties and responsibilities of adult life, it causes brutality, neglect, and a never ending round of untold squalor and misery. The sum total of human suffering caused by drunken parents is immeasurable. Certainly it is more than that arising from all other causes combined. The army of individuals reared under such circumstances are savages real as any with which our soldiers on the frontier ever had to deal; but they are savages of a lower type than those. They are constantly at war with the better interests of humanity as exemplified in a progressive, civilized society, for they respect neither personal nor property rights.

Not through drunkenness alone, as that term is popularly understood, but also through "moderate drinking" is the average moral tone, the average capability for exercising the subtlest mental processes through which fine distinctions of right and wrong conduct are determined, immeasurably lowered. The human brain, through countless centuries of evolutionary progress has acquired a fineness of texture, a sensitiveness to external impressions and a corresponding swiftness of function, which make it the most powerful and at the same time the most easily injured of all animal organs. It is just upon this fineness of brain texture that civilization depends for the carrying out of her highest aims and purposes, for the solution of the manifold and complicated problems which social progress is bringing forth on every hand; and it is this same fineness of brain texture that is destroyed or rendered impossible of development under the influence of even "moderate" quantities of alcohol daily ingested.

To the individual no less than to the state are the irritating and stupefying effects of alcohol an irreparable loss. The same degree of brain development which makes the citizen's voice and conduct of such value to the state also renders him capable of enjoying the greatest degree of human happiness, a healthy enjoyment of the purely physical pleasures of life and that exquisite happiness born of a healthy contemplation of the subtleties of natural phenomena, of the development of human progress as exhibited in history, the intricacies of mechanical problems, or any other department of human knowledge which may especially engage his attention. All of these are a mental *Terra Incognita* to the man who daily takes his measure of alcoholic beverage, even though it may never be sufficient to make him noticeably drunk. Civilization, moreover, suffers immeasurable loss through the corrupting influence of the liquor traffic upon the affairs of government. So widespread and intricate is its contamination in this respect that nearly every great municipality in our country has been compelled to recognize it as a power, and protect it in its destructive and corrupting business. In many instances it has succeeded in getting entire control of the affairs of government, and these cases have always been attended by retrogression and disaster to human progress.

Alcohol exerts its corrupting influence beyond those who drink it. Its evils act as examples to corrupt the impressionable of all classes. The saloon attracts not only those who are inclined to drink, but all kinds and grades of evildoers. It is as truly the pest spot for the development of crime as is the sewage contaminated well the source of typhoid fever. Is a murder, a highway robbery, a burglary, to be committed, it is almost always planned in a private room of a saloon. So are the numberless petty crimes by organized gangs of human vultures who prey upon the industrious public.

In short, the universal consumption of these alcoholic poisons render impossible the realization of civilization's highest ideals. It does this because it destroys a vast number of useful lives, renders many more physically incompetent through disease, destroys an immense amount of valuable brain matter annually, increases insanity, incurs the expense of supporting a vast army of non-producers, immeasurably increases crime, brings unhappiness, poverty, and misery to millions, and causes a corrupt administration of the affairs of government. I firmly believe that we have in this great country of ours a system of government, natural resources, and a people of the kind to give to the world in fifty years, if the production and importation of alcoholic beverages were absolutely prohibited, a people that for beauty, strength, virtue, material wealth, and happiness would equal the fondest dreams of a Millennium.

XX.

What is the Best Method of Dealing with the Alcoholic Question.

It is not the purpose of this work to give even a brief history of the various temperance and prohibition movements which have been inaugurated from time to time, both in Europe and in America, to abate the evils of alcoholic poisoning. All of the movements have received attention by other writers; and especially have the legislative aspects of the liquor problem in America received adequate treatment in a carefully prepared volume by Dr. F. H. Wines and Mr. John Koven, of the "Committee of Fifty" (The Liquor Problem in Its Legislative Aspects, by F. H. Wines and John Koven, 1897). The general statement may be made that all temperance movements, whether lay, religious, or legislative, have accomplished some good; but sometimes the amount of good accomplished has been very small compared with the efforts put forth; and it has oftentimes seemed that the same amount of effort applied in a different direction might have been productive of greater results.

Particularly interesting and instructive has been the inauguration of legislative prohibition and governmental control of the liquor traffic, by giving the state the sole right of dispensing alcoholic liquors. The history of all legislative prohibition shows that while the real prohibition which the law sought to attain has never yet actually been accomplished, the enactment of all prohibitory laws has been attended by some measure of good, the amount being in exact ratio with the fidelity with which the laws were enforced. Where public opinion has been in favor of their enforcement a practical degree of prohibition has been attained; but public opinion is unstable, and the community which is earnest in its desire for a total supression of the liquor traffic this year may not be of the same opinion next year; so the prohibitory laws are contravened with impunity and fall into disrepute. In many communities in which the state has assumed the functions of the liquor dispenser a notable improvement in public morals has resulted. This improvement has been due to the fact that the cupidity of the saloonkeeper, who seeks by every means in his power to sell as much as possible, is removed, liquor being dispensed only in a certain quantity and not at all to any one who has the reputation of being a drunkard. Moreover, the officials in charge of the state dispensaries, having no interest in the sale of the liquor, and their terms of office depending upon the fidelity with which the laws regulating the sale are carried out, they attend strictly and faithfully to all the legal details which rob the traffic as far as possible of its evil influences. Moreover, the state dispensary system has decreased the number of saloons, in some communities entirely abolishing them, decreasing in the same degree their corrupting influences; and the one dispensary which has displaced the many saloons is a model of decency compared with the average saloon. The dispensary, too, does a great deal for abstinence in making social drinking impossible. The man who patronizes the dispensary gets the poison for his own consumption, so that only one person is injured thereby. If he patronizes a saloon, the chances are many to one that his social instincts would cause at least another person to indulge who would not have done so otherwise. It is likely, too, that the moral teachings of the dispensary may be of value to boys and young men. An institution around which the state has fixed so many limitations must appeal to the intelligence of the average youth as being an evil. Certainly alcohol under such restrictions has none of the charm which attends its sale in the midst of gay company, with games and music, and surrounded by the expensive lavishness of fine furniture, cut glass, and the other attractions which give to the liquor traffic its greatest fascination, and an appearance of well being and cleanliness which it little deserves.

The value of the dispensary system in comparison with laws totally prohibiting all traffic in alcoholic beverages is well illustrated in the experience of Sweden with the well-known "Gothenburg system." The system was named from the town in which it was first inaugurated, in 1871. The beneficial effects of this method of dealing with the alcohol question are seen in the results obtained. In 1891 there were only 304 places in the entire country where spirits could be bought, that is, one place to every 6,600 inhabitants; and the per capita consumption of absolute alcohol fell from the enormous quantity of 8 liters, or over two gallons, to 1.8 liters. In 1890, however, a new law was passed which was much more stringent in its operations than the one it superseded. It completely abolished the still existing small private sale of liquor, and almost suppressed the sale of spirits in the entire country; forbade among other things all sale of liquor from one o'clock Saturday afternoon until eight o'clock Monday morning, and on all other days of the week before eight o'clock in the morning. Moreover, it gave local option to the cities, the inhabitants having the power to decide by ballot whether they would continue under the state dispensary system or have total prohibition. All persons, whether

BEST METHOD OF SUPPRESSING ALCOHOL. 205

male or female, over twenty-five years of age were entitled to vote on the question. In fourteen cities the result was for total prohibition, the women by the earnestness with which they carried on the campaign contributing much to the result.

The experiment of prohibition in Sweden has, however, not been a success. No sooner did it become impossible to purchase spirits openly than was an illicit trade begun; in spite of the efforts of the authorities, those who wished to purchase alcoholic liquors found some way of doing so. Liquors were surreptitiously brought into the territory from which they had by popular voice been expelled and small stills were erected in many places for their manufacture. Indeed, the demoralization engendered by the unlawful traffic has been so great that many cities which had voted for prohibition have returned or contemplate returning to the restricted traffic under the dispensary system.

It will thus be seen that attempts to entirely suppress all trade in spirituous liquors has been attended by the same results in Sweden as those with which we are familiar in America.

Perhaps the greatest hindrance to the total suppression of commercial traffic in alcoholic liquors is the power of the invested capital engaged in their production. At the present time over four hundred million dollars are invested in the breweries of the United States alone. Certainly as much more is engaged in the production of spirits and wine. Add to this the value of the land which is constantly engaged in supplying grain and fruit as raw material to the beverage manufacturing establishments and the amout of capital engaged, directly or indirectly, must be considerably more than one thousand million dollars. The value of the annual product of the breweries, based on the estimates for 1895, is not less than two hundred million dollars, and of spirits and wine not less than one hundred million dollars' worth are sold annually. Thus the products of the breweries, distilleries, and wine presses for 1895 had a wholesale value of more than three hundred million dollars, while the combined value of the wheat and corn crops of that year was only two hundred thirty-seven million dollars.

Moreover, the capital invested in the production of alcoholic beverages is more active and aggressive than that interested in the carrying on of any other enterprise. Not only do individual brewers and distillers have to meet the ordinary competition of others in the same business, but they constantly keep at work some political force such as will enable them to influence legislation favorable to their cause. The extent of the brewers' influence in some municipalities probably outweighs the combined influence of the rest of the citizens. Certainly it is sufficient to determine the direction of alcohol legislation. Speaking of this state of affairs in the city of St. Louis the authors of "The Liquor Problem in Its Legislative Aspects" make the following statement (Pp. 331 and 332): "The multiplication of dram shops is largely due to the business rivalry between breweries, of which St. Louis has twenty-five or thirty, some of them among the largest in the United States, if not in the world. Three-fourths at least of the saloons are indirectly owned and operated by the breweries, which advance the license tax and collect it in installments by charging eight dollars a barrel for beer instead of six." In the city of Boston a similar state of affairs exists. Quoting from the same book (P. 192) we find that: "The small liquor shop keepers were controlled by their bondsmen, largely brewers and wholesale dealers, and readily did the bidding of the latter for the protection enjoyed or from necessity. In fact, the liquor power at this time was virtually a few men's power. In 1894, for instance, twenty-five wholesale dealers were sureties for 1,030 saloonkeepers. Three brewers were on 328 bonds, another was on 112, others on from 8 to 109 each. Twenty-five men thus had assumed a monied liability of $2,660,000, some of them a liability in excess of the value of their property."

In Chicago, Milwaukee, and other large centers of population the influence of the brewer, distiller, and wholesaler is similarly exerted.

It is seen, therefore, that the enormous capital concerned in manufacturing alcoholic beverages exerts its whole influence along such lines as will tend to promote the sale of its products and prevent interference on the part of municipal authorities by keeping an army of dependents which efficiently checks all projected unfavorable legislation.

To meet and overcome the aggressive energy of the makers and dispensers of alcoholic liquors, needs first of all a proper education on the part of the people. Something of the kind is now going on with the children in the public schools, and undoubtedly much good is being accomplished thereby; but the system has many faults. The nature of the information thus imparted is often inaccurate and exaggerated. Recently a so-called "health primer" was brought to the writer's notice, which exemplified this faulty teaching. It was a "popular" treatise on physiology, inaccurate in its statements, unattractive in its style of expression, and the subject of alcohol was dragged in at the end of each lesson, in an absurd attempt to "point a moral or adorn a tale." Yet this method had the approval of a professor of medicine in one of our largest Universities, and was adopted in the schools of one of our wealthiest and most populous states through the influence of the superintendent of public instruction.

The child who would carry home to a beer-drinking father the statement that "beer changes the inside coat of the stomach into leather" would be liable to have all the useful information he might acquire at school regarding the bad effects of alcohol neutralized by the superior wisdom of the father. Indeed, I have before me now several letters written by irate fathers to teachers of public schools, in which these anti-alcohol teachings have been resented with much warmth, going so far even as personal abuse of the teacher. Let the truth be told about alcohol and alcoholic beverages to those children whom we would teach to avoid them, and no generous nature will, in mature years, resent the teachings of his childhood and discard it all as false.

But the education of the children alone is not sufficient. Some form of popular education should be inaugurated. In England scientific subjects were popularized and knowledge concerning them imparted by lecture. Workingmen's clubs listened with delight to popular lectures on scientific subjects given by Huxley, Tyndal, Darwin, Herbert Spencer, and others; and though there never can be another Huxley, Tyndal, nor Darwin, every community of a few thousand inhabitants has one or more persons capable of treating the subject of alcohol from a scientific standpoint and at the same time making it interesting and easily understood. Let the subject be taught experimentally, as far as possible, demonstrating the falsity of the belief that alcohol gives strength or that beer is a valuable food, or that any of the alcoholic beverages have a tonic value. Surely the intelligent workingman who now spends from ten to twenty-five per cent of his daily wages for beer because he believes that beer has a high food value would not spend the pittance which is so sorely needed by his family if he were convinced that in buying beer he is paying from ten to twenty times what he would have to pay for the same food in the form of bread. Nor would he end his substantial midday meal with a large glass of raw whiskey, as I have frequently seen him do, if he knew that he was thereby diminishing his strength and decreasing his digestive powers in a notable degree. Much of this kind of education should come from the medical profession. No thoughtful medical man will prescribe a drug so potent for evil as alcohol without being first assured that it meet the indications for which it is prescribed. He should not say to his patient "get a case of beer" or "get a case of wine" or spirits any more than he would say "get a pound of opium" or chloroform or chloral or any other dangerous narcotic. Let him know the truth about alcohol and prescribe it as he would any other narcotic of its class, warning his patient against its dangers and explaining to him the popular errors regarding alcoholic beverages which have found credence and have passed uncontradicted from time immemorial. Let him tell the wealthy owner of a valuable winecellar who is the victim of Bright's disease or the father of an imbecile child or inebriate son that his cherished winecellar is responsible for all his misfortune. It is nonsense to deny that thousands of useful, brilliant professional men and business men are yearly cut off in the very prime of their prosperity and usefulness by some disease engendered by a habit of daily alcohol imbibition, and who go to their graves not knowing the origin of their illness. The physician sees and knows (or should know), but he is silent. He may adopt the old English phrase and call it "high living"; but it is alcoholic degeneration.

Temperance advocates are wont to base their arguments on moral or moral-ethical grounds, neglecting the purely scientific side of the argument. The wisdom of this method is doubtful. Undoubtedly alcoholic excess is immoral and contravenes man's ethical relations to his fellows; but it should be remembered that the social-ethical sense is first to be destroyed in alcoholic degeneration. To undertake to rouse the drunkard, therefore, by pointing out the sufferings of others which his conduct entails is not so liable to succeed as would the conviction that his excesses must speedily end in death.

While education of the people as to the exact nature and value of all alcoholic beverages may do much to bring about a total suppression of the liquor traffic, it alone will not be sufficient to do so. A multitude of people would drink and get drunk, even if they knew that alcohol possessed no value beyond its intoxicating effects and that the drinking thereof might be followed by dangerous or fatal disease. Great evils, too, are protected and propagated by the very inertia of custom and precedent. The evils of slavery were recognized at the time of the adoption of the constitution and measures taken to suppress the importation of slaves after 1808; but more than a half-century later a bloody and costly war was necessary to destroy that hideous institution. Traffic in alcoholic liquors will be tolerated for the same reason—the indisposition of the great mass of influential conservative citizens to interfere with established institutions—long after the people are educated to their worthlessness and dangers.

The whole tide of public opinion must be changed. At the present time, in the average community, while there may be several shades of opinion as to the value of the different alcoholic liquors, nowhere is it considered positively immoral nor even reprehensible to partake of any form of alcohol drink "in moderation." The average public opinion looks upon it as a matter of course everywhere excepting in comparatively unimportant localities, and these are treated by most people with a considerable measure of contempt. It is curious to note the different standards of morality which individuals make for themselves in their different treatment of the alcohol question. There are certain men who have their liquors shipped to their residences who would feel degraded if seen drinking in a saloon. Others will drink a home-made wine containing fifteen or twenty per cent of alcohol, who would look upon a bottle of five or six per cent wine from the wine merchant with abhorrence. A multitude of similar idiosyncrasies may be discovered with little trouble. There is, it is true, an undercurrent of feeling that the drinking of liquors, especially the stronger alcoholic liquors, is not entirely creditable. I have before me an advertisement for a whiskey, which I clipped, by the way, from a church paper, in which the would-be purchaser is assured that "we ship in plain packages—no marks to indicate contents (which will avoid possible comment)." The same desire not to be caught in the act of drinking accounts for the curtains always drawn and the screened bars of the saloon. But this tacit understanding that the drinking of alcoholic beverages is an evil has come to be regarded, like all the other evils of alcohol consumption, as a matter of course. It seems to have very little influence in the direction of creating a public opinion sufficiently strong to inaugurate a movement for suppressing the evil.

Our code of morals, however, will not permit us to regard the taking of opium with the same degree of equanimity. As has been elsewhere remarked, if anyone should enter into the business of dispensing pleasant tasting beverages having morphine, cocaine, hasheesh, or some other narcotic than alcohol, for their active principle, how outraged the community would be, and if severe punishment were meted out to the originator of the enterprise, it would be greeted with universal approval. The man, too, who habitually visits an "opium den" is shunned by his fellows and talked about with superstitious horror. This same man might go to an "alcohol den" a score of times every day without losing his reputation as a gentleman, or the regard of his fellow men. This is simply because we are accustomed to seeing men indulge in alcoholic instead of other narcotic beverages. Let there be created a public opinion against the indulgence in all forms of narcotics, alcohol included, such as that which now exists against the indulgence in opium, and the liquor traffic will easily be abolished.

Of greatest influence in perpetuating the custom of drinking alcoholic beverages is the important part which they play in the social intercourse of modern society, and especially in the everyday exchange of civilities between men of all kinds of business and all professions. To be invited to partake of some kind of alcoholic drink immediately opens the way to business negotiations, brushing away at once that reserve which makes the meeting of strangers more or less unpleasant, and opening up the way to a more intimate friendship. Moreover, custom has made the offering of a glass of wine one of the first duties of domestic hospitality with a vast majority of civilized people. Indeed, this custom, through centuries of recognition by the world's most enlightened people, has become so essentially a part of our civilization that it will be the most difficult to abolish of all the causes which promote alcohol drinking. It would seem that something of the kind is an absolute necessity. Yet what is there that can be made to take the place of alcoholic beverages which will be more acceptable? Undoubtedly coffee houses and other places where non-alcoholic drinks may be had, reading and lectures rooms and others in which games may be played are doing much to supply the medium of social intercourse, but a great deal of energy must be expended before they are made to totally supplant the saloon and winecellar. High license and all other restrictive legislation which public opinion will allow to be adequately carried out should be earnestly supported until such time as alcohol for human consumption will be found only on the shelves of the apothecary and will be dispensed only upon the physician's prescription and only in such cases as call for sedative or narcotic treatment.

As to the treatment of drunkenness, inebriety, and all pathological conditions arising from irritating effects of alcohol, each case is a separate problem and requires the intelligent handling of the skilled physician. Removal of patient from his surroundings, withdrawal of alcohol, support to the functions of nutrition, sedation for the nervous system, until such time as the normal physiological processes are re-established, with proper protection against associations or nerve storms which would lead to renewing the habit, are the chief considerations.

INDEX.

A

	Page.
Abstinence and Expectations in Life Insurance	192
Adulterations of Alcoholic Beverages, Popular Belief in	169–171
Adulterations of Wine	31
Adulterations of Beer	33–34
Adulterations of Spirits	34–36
Aggressiveness of Liquor Traffic	205
Alcoholic Excess Among Ancient Germans	17–20
Alcoholic Excess Among Germans in Middle Ages	20–25
Alcoholic Excess in England	24–25
Alcoholic Excess Present Day	25
Alcohol, Oxidation in the Body	31 et seq.
Alcohol, Elimination of	41
Alcohol, Affinity for Oxygen	42
Alcohol Not a Carbohydrate Food	43–44
Alcohol in U. S. Army	56
Alcohol in Morbidity and Mortality in Switzerland	191
Ancient History of Wine Making	9
Ancient History of Beer Making	10–11
Assimilation, Effects of Alcohol upon	70
Austria, Alcoholic Insanity in	123–124

B

Beer, Adulterations of	34–36
Beer, Amount of Alcohol in	34
Beer, Constituents of	34
Beer, Contains no Diastase	164
Beer Drinking and Inebriety	184
Beer Drunkard, Appearance of	164
Beer, Evils of Drinking	183
Beer Compared with Bread, Food Value of	46–47
Beer, German contains more Sugar than American	164
Beer, Material used for Coloring	36
Beer Making Among Germans, Growth of	19

INDEX—CONTINUED.

	Page.
Beer, Popular Estimation of	163
Beer Produces Unlimited Drunkenness	163
Beer, Stomach Troubles Produced by	166
Beer, Why It increases Bodily Weight	163–164
Belief That Alcohol is a Natural Stimulant	172
Boquet of Wine, What ?	168
Brewing Among Ancient Central Americans	14–15
Brewing Among Ancient Egyptians	10
Brewing Among Ancient Greeks	11
Brewing Among Ancient Mexicans	12
Brewing Among Polynesians	17
Brewing Among Romans	12
Brewing Among South Americans	15–16

C

Careless Prescribing of Alcohol	175
Character, Effects of Alcohol Upon	95 et seq.
Children, Effects of Alcohol Upon	101–102
Chemical Effects of Alcohol on Digestion	67
Cholera, Susceptibility Increased by Alcohol	67–72
Commercial Inebriate Cures	157–158
Consumption of Alcohol in Europe	189
Corruption of Municipal Affairs by Alcohol	200–201
Crime, Relation to Alcoholism	193 et seq.
Crime, Committed by "Occasional Drunkards"	195
Crime, Committed by "Constant Drunkards"	195–197
Crime, Amount for which Alcohol is Responsible	197–198
Crime, Days of Week upon which Committed	197

D

Degeneration of Nerve Cells, Alcoholic	93–94
Digestion, Effects of Alcohol upon	66 et seq.
Diseases, Alcohol in Treatment of	129
Dispensaries, Government	202
Drunkards, Reasons for More Males	140
Drunkards, Social Influences in Making	139
Drunkards, Who Become	139–140
Drunkenness Among Germans in the XVI Century	20–25
Drunkenness in England in XVIII Century	23–24
Drunkenness, A Bar to Progress	198
Drunkenness, A Cause of Human Misery	198

E

	Page.
Education Concerning Alcohol, Popular	208
Elimination of Alcohol	41
Embryo, Effects of Alcohol Upon	104–108
Excretion of Oxidized Products of Alcohol	43
Exhaustion, Heart, In Alcoholism	83–86
Ethics of Opium and Alcohol Indulgence	213

F

Families, Alcoholic, Soon Run Out	115
Fatigue, Effects of Alcohol Upon	160
Fermentation, By-Products of	171
Food Value of Beer vs. Bread	46–47
France, Alcoholic Insanity in	111–112
France, Increase of Alcoholic Consumption in	123

G

Gambrinus, Origin of	26
Gas, Exchange Affected by Alcohol	74
Germany, Alcoholic Insanity in	122–123
Germany, Prevalence of Alcoholic Poisoning in	124
Glycogenic Functions Affected by Alcohol	72
Gothenburg System	204–205

H

Habitual Drinkers and Total Abstainers, Different Effects of Alcohol upon	72–73
Heart Diseases of Alcoholism	83 et seq.
Heart Exhaustion of Alcoholism	83–86
Heart in Alcoholism, Chronic Diseases of	86
Heart Dilatation	87–88
Heredity, Influence of Alcohol upon	103–116
Home Drinking, Ethics of	211
Hops, Substitutes For	35

I

Illness Due to Alcohol, Amount of	189–190
Inebriety, What ?	141
Inebriety, Constant	152
Inebriety, Constant, Causes of	152
Inebriety, Former Punishment For	142

INDEX—CONTINUED.

	Page.
Inebriety, Periodic	145–151
Inebriety, Popular Interpretation of	142
Inebriety, Real and Pseudo	143–144
Inebriate, Constant Not Always a Degenerate	154
Inebriates, Alcoholic Degeneracy of	108–111
Inebriates, Criminal Tendencies of	113
Immunity Against Alcoholic Poisoning	114
Insanity, Alcoholic	117–127
Insanity, Alcoholic, Statistics of	117–122
Insanity, Alcoholic, in Massachusetts	119–121
Insanity, Alcoholic, in Germany	122–123
Insanity, Alcoholic, in France	123
Insanity, Alcoholic, in Austria	123–124
Insanity, Alcoholic, Among German Children	125–126

K

Kidney, Alcoholic Diseases of	89

L

Liquor Traffic, Aggressiveness of	205
Liquor Traffic, Suppression of	202
Liquor Traffic, Loss Entailed by	187–188
Liquor Traffic, Power of	205–206
Liver, Alcoholic Diseases of	90
Loss to State Through Drunkenness	200

M

Malt in Beer, Substitutes For	34–35
Malt Liquors and Wine, Comparative Effects of	168
Malt Liquors, Increase in Consumption of	182
Medicine, Alcohol as a	174
Mental Processes, Effects of Alcohol Upon	57 et seq.
Metabolism, Effects of Alcohol Upon	71
Moderate Drinking, Bar to Highest Happiness	198
Money Spent for Alcoholic Drinks	184–186
Morel's Table of Alcoholic Degeneration	113
Motor Disturbances of Alcoholism	98–99
Mortality, Alcoholic, in Switzerland	191–192
Morbidity, Alcoholic, in English Army	192
Municipal Affairs and Alcohol	200–201
Muscular Contractions Affected by Alcohol	49 et seq.

	Page.
Muscular Movements of Stomach Affected by Alcohol	69

N

Narcotic, Alcohol an Inferior	175-176
Nerve Cells in Alcoholism, Degeneration of	93-94
Nerve Tissue, Effects of Alcohol upon	91-94

O

Opium and Alcoholic Indulgence, Ethics of	212
Oxygen, Affinity of Alcohol for	42

P

Paralysis in Alcoholism	99-100
Periodic Drunkards	145-151
Peripheral Nerves in Alcoholism, Degeneration of	100
Peripheral Nerves of Stomach, Effects of Alcohol upon	69
Physicians Duty to Public in the Use of Alcohol	209
Per Capita Consumption of Alcohol	178, 189
Popular Errors about Alcoholic Beverages	159 at seq.
Popular Estimate of Wine	166
Popular Belief in Adulterations	169-171
Popular Education about Alcohol	211-212
Physicians and The Value of Alcohol	128-138
Physicians and The Use of Alcohol 50 years Ago	129
Physicians, Recent Opinions Favorable to Alcohol	131-136
Proteid Metabolism, Affected by Alcohol	71
Ptyalin, Effects of Alcohol Upon	71
Prohibition, Difficulty of Obtaining	203

R

Reformation of Drunkards, Accidental	155-156
Resistance, Tissue, Decreased by Alcohol	75
Russia, Drunkenness Among Children of	126

S

Saloon, Evil Influences of	201
Saloon, Substitutes for	213
Schools, Temperance Taught in	207
Social Drinking in Producing Inebriety, Effects of	145-146
Special Senses in Alcohol, Disturbances of	98
Spirits, Adulterations of	33-34
Spirits, Constituents of	31-33

	Page.
Spirits, Materials to Color	33
Stimulant, What it is	48
Stimulant, Alcohol not, in Chloroform Narcosis	54
Stimulates, How Alcohol	55 et seq.
State by Drunkenness, Loss to	200
Stomach, Effects of Alcohol Upon	66–69
Stomach Troubles Produced by Beer	166
Sugar Compared with Alcohol, Food Value of	46
Suppression of Liquor Traffic	202
Switzerland, Mortality Statistics of	191

T

Temperance Taught in Schools	207
Temperature, Effects of Alcohol upon	161
Temperance Hospital, London	174
Tissue Resistance Decreased by Alcohol	75 et seq.
Tissue, How Broken Down by Alcohol	103
Toxicity of Alcohol	177
Tuberculosis and Alcoholism	78 et seq.

W

Wine Drinking Among Early Germans	17
Wine Making, Origin of	10
Wine, Constituents of	29–31
Wine, Adulterations of	31
Wine, Materials Used in Coloring	31
Wine, Old, Popular Estimation of	166

www.ingramcontent.com/pod-product-compliance
Lightning Source LLC
Chambersburg PA
CBHW021820230426
43669CB00008B/810